CONTROL YOURSELF

David R. Wheeler

CONTROL YOURSELF

Nelson-Hall
Chicago

LIBRARY OF CONGRESS CATALOGING IN PUBLICATION DATA

Wheeler, David R
  Control yourself.

  Includes index.
  1. Self-control.   I. Title
BF632.W48   158'.1   76-15259
ISBN 0-88229-207-2

Copyright © 1976 by David R. Wheeler

All rights reserved. No part of this book may be reproduced in any form without permission in writing from the publisher, except by a reviewer who wishes to quote brief passages in connection with a review written for broadcast or for inclusion in a magazine or newspaper. For information address Nelson-Hall Inc., Publishers, 325 W. Jackson Blvd., Chicago, Illinois 60606.

Manufactured in the United States of America.

Contents

1   Self-control   1
2   The permanent power of self-control   9
3   Why change?   15
4   The principles of self-control   23
5   Positive consequences   37
6   Negative consequences   47
7   Environmental self-control   59
8   Control your health   71
9   Biological monitoring and feedback   85
10 Fears and phobias   91
11 Relaxation and self-hypnosis   105
12 Control your creativity   121
13 Modifying your intellect   131
14 The self-control of your success   145
15 Controlling your bad habits   153
16 A better life through self-control   163
    Notes and references   169
    Index   175

1

Self-control

You can control yourself, Anything that you do, feel, or think can be modified and controlled on your own. Behavior ranging from habitual nail-biting to intellectual creativity can be altered.

This is a do-it-yourself book. Just as easily as you can learn to paint a picture by numbers, you can learn the principles of self-control. The control of yourself is possible without the need for reliance on anyone but yourself. This book presents an effective and proven method for self-improvement. It will become your own personal program formulated to your specific needs. You set your goals and you control yourself.

The search for self-improvement seems to be popular considering the large number of self-help books and articles that are currently available. The rate of dropping out from these programs usually approaches 100 percent. Few of the behavioral changes resulting from the use of other self-help programs last for more than a week or two. For some reason people revert to their old way of doing things. As an example, one has only to look at the number of fad diets that are attempted and discarded. Some self-improvement books are so vague that many individuals cannot even begin their programs much less make the changes in their lives permanent.

Until recently self-improvement books have lacked experimentally proven and viable techniques. Contained in this book are methods for controlling yourself. You are free to select anything about yourself that you want to change and then modify it with the simple principles in this book.

This book is unlike any other self-improvement book because the skills and techniques for control are so easy to establish and to use. Once you have begun the modification of some aspect of your behavior, the techniques require so little effort that you enjoy the changes in your life.

One of the major reasons for the failures of many programs for self-control has been the lack of specific instructions. Some statements—"You need only to think success in order to become successful," or "Think money and you shall become rich"—are just too vague to be of much help in controlling one's self. You cannot create a great chef merely by putting that label on a person. Behavior change just does not work that way. Giving people recipes and teaching them how to use them are the ways to develop culinary experts. In much the same manner as one learns to be a great cook, one can be taught self-improvement. The basic skills of self-control are taught in this book.

Success, happiness, proper attitudes, and self-control are usually assumed to be a result of a mixture of luck and heredity, not of learned skills and techniques. If you believe this, then it means that you either have or have not got what it takes to improve yourself. There is nothing you can do to change your station in life. I feel that failures in self-control are not due to a lack of innate ability, or luck, or even some exploitable natural talent, but that people have not been shown the procedures that result in long-lasting and effective self-control. This book reveals those procedures that can bring about self-control.

With the techniques found in this book you select what you want to control, you monitor your own controls, and you devise your self-improvement program. The instructions in the following chapters have been written to help you help yourself. You will experience a gradual but permanent change. Likely you will never finish this self-improvement program because of the new goals you will continually set for yourself based on your previous successes with this program.

SELF-CONTROL DEVELOPMENTS

The program for your self-control presented in this book is structured around the area of psychology known as behavior modification. To understand the principles of modifying behavior, I shall briefly trace the major historical events leading up to the present techniques.

Psychology can be roughly divided into two broad classification schemes. One is the cognitive viewpoint, which is concerned with such things as thinking, creativity, emotions, and meaning. The second classification has become known as Stimulus-Response (S-R). S-R psychologists treat as legitimate areas of inquiry only those things that can be seen, measured directly, weighed, or counted in some manner.

Cognitive and stimulus-response psychologists study learning although with differing approaches. A cognitive view of learning has to do with the organism acquiring a disposition to make a proper response. In terms of S-R theorists, learning has to do with probability that behaviors will occur as a result of reinforcements and training.

A form of learning known as classical conditioning was experimentally tested by Ivan Pavlov at the start of this century. Pavlov was a Russian physiologist who, in the process of studying the processes of digestion, discovered the relationship between a stimulus and a response. Classical conditioning theory attempts to show why a stimulus elicits a response.

Pavlov experimented with dogs. The normal reflex for a hungry dog when exposed to the sight of food is salivation. By accident, Pavlov noticed that whenever he presented some other stimulus along with the food for a long enough period of time, the nonfood stimulus would also elicit salivation without the food being present. Pavlov was thus able to condition the dog to salivate to the ringing of a bell. Needless to say, without the association of the bell and the food, conditioning a salivation response to the bell would have been impossible.

An offshoot of classical conditioning was the work done by John Watson during the 1920s and the 1930s. Watson's approach utilized the concepts of a stimulus and a response, but he was opposed to the cognitive theories of human behavior. He was concerned only with physiological reactions. He rejected introspection as a method of observation. He replaced cognition, emotions, thinking, and other "mentalistic" processes with observable behavior. Watson became widely known because of his infamous remarks about his ability to mold children into any kind of persons that he wanted them to become.

The techniques of operant conditioning grew out of the work and ideas of Pavlov and Watson. Behavior modification techniques have been borrowed from operant-conditioning techniques. Operant conditioning is concerned with the conditions under which some response can be made to occur or the circumstances that bring about a change in the rate of responding. Behavior modification is concerned with the relationships between changes in the environment and the corresponding effects on a person's responses. Behavior is influenced by the surroundings in which such responses occur.

Operant-conditioning techniques are effective in controlling, modifying, and maintaining a wide range of behavior. Behavior modification teaches us how to apply the powerful tools of operant conditioning for use in a program for self-control. The essence of the approach is to structure and arrange the conditions surrounding the behavior that you want to change.

The techniques of behavioral control are available to anyone wishing to spend a few weeks in researching the many academic journals. Practicing psychologists have been reluctant to translate their findings into a program that an individual can use on his own. It is not that they do not work, but professional considerations have made it difficult to bring the techniques to the public's attention. Since these techniques were developed and used in clinical situations, psychologists have hesitated in allowing people to administer training to themselves in an unsupervised manner. Until now, the power to control human behavior has resided in the hands of psychologists; but, self-management and self-control of one's own behavior are the most efficient and durable method. With behavior-modification principles you can control yourself.

An Eclectic Approach to Self-Control

The self-control program that I present in this book uses an eclectic approach. Although I have based the framework of your self-improvement program on the principles of behavior modification, I have also incorporated the rich insights from cognitive psychologists. The program allows the use of almost any other method of self-improvement.

Although there is a difference in the theoretical views of cognitive and behavioral (or stimulus–response) schools of psychology, I believe that to ignore one or the other is wrong. Experimental behaviorists talk of recordable, overt actions, and they do not like to use cognitive labels such as "love" or "hate." An enduring kiss to a behaviorist is merely a set of muscular constrictions; but, we feel many mental states that are not observed by others. Just because someone else does not witness their occurrence does not mean that the feelings are not real to us. A cognitive understanding is also necessary if we are to develop a complete understanding of ourselves. An eclectic approach that samples the best and most effective principles from several sources is the best method for developing a complete program for your self-improvement. Anything that will allow you to control your destiny should be the criterion for the selection of self-control techniques. It is only of passing concern that the techniques may come from different areas of psychology.

Many people find it impossible to believe that they can develop the will power to control their own behavior and become the masters of their own fates. You probably have heard the following statement several times before—"I've tried to quit smoking, but I just couldn't do it." The speaker is making it appear that some external force is causing his behavior. He is saying that it is the cigarette that will not let him stop smoking. This is a belief, which is shared by many others, that only external controllers have the necessary power to control our behavior.

This is an incorrect viewpoint. A moment's reflection should convince you of the real ineffectiveness of having external controls placed on individual behavior. Prisons do not change the behavior of individuals for long once they leave the institutions. People may seek the help of psychiatrists, and they may spend years in the treatment. Torture and brainwashing are never effective in changing attitudes of those who are exposed to these external "treatments." Even money given for working does not cause the assembly-line worker to be any happier with his job. Outside influences on your behavior, attitudes, and personality are never as effective in control as are your own internal regulators. Your feelings of self-esteem are more likely to modify your self-improvement behavior than are physical punishments delivered to you by someone else. A program for self-control must reside within you if it is to work and continue to be effective.

The self-improvement program presented in the following chapters is self-sufficient. You can change yourself permanently without the help of time-consuming and costly professionals. My idea in the development and writing of this book was to cut through the technical jargon of the academic journals and to present in an understandable manner the framework for a self-help program that would fit the needs of everyone.

Medical doctors, bankers, lawyers, hypnotists, and anyone else you believe would benefit you in your quest for self-control may be consulted. This will not upset the efficiency of the self-improvement program, and it may even improve the program. You will be totally free to pick and choose whatever portions you think will be of the most immediate benefit to you. This program in self-control will show you how to reach the goals you have set for yourself. Other self-help books may be consulted and incorporated into this generalized self-control program.

Although developed from clinical research, behavior-modifying techniques have been used successfully in nonclinical situations. Students have been able to modify their studying, to stop smoking, to control drinking problems, and to eliminate their sexual problems with the techniques of behavior modification.

Maybe you have tried to improve yourself, but nothing was actually accomplished. You probably tried hard to improve, but gave up when you saw no improvement. What went wrong? Other self-improvement courses seem to ignore the most important catalyst in any self-improvement program. This is a program that is tailored to fit you exactly.

Now with this book it will be possible to fit a self-control program exactly to your individual needs and requirements. All you have to do is to read and apply the principles and techniques that are outlined. These newly applied skills will literally open a fresh world of personal accomplishment.

The techniques for self-improvement will not work overnight. You would not expect to alter a lifetime's worth of bad habits with the swiftness of taking a pill. But the techniques of behavior modification will bring about gradual *but* lasting improvements.

This program for self-control will do at least one thing for you that other programs have not done—it will allow *you* to guide yourself. *You* select your goals, *you* fit the self-controls to your style of life, and *you* become the master of your own destiny.

2

The permanent power of self-control

The changes in one's behavior brought about by operant-conditioning techniques can be permanent if you so desire. The power of these controls will be effective in bringing about modifications in any behavior. The critical arrangement of rewards and one's environment (both of these important principles of behavior modification are presented in subsequent chapters) can form strong, desirable habits and break lifelong bad habits.

I shall present some examples in this chapter to illustrate the potency and the permanency of simple operant-conditioning techniques. Operant behaviors are either strengthened by rewards or weakened by negative reinforcers that *follow* the response. Thus, it can be said that operant behavior is controlled by its consequences (the effects of its occurrence). In this chapter the attainment of self-control will be discussed in terms of the relationship of behavior to the environment. The conditioning of permanent behavioral changes for purposes of self-control will also be explored. The following examples may help to convince you that no matter how long you may have had them or how strong you may think that they are, simple operant-conditioning techniques are even more powerful. Once established and practiced, the behavioral techniques *will* work for you.

Permanent Effects

Once taught with operant techniques, learned behaviors seem to be permanent. During World War II, pigeons were conditioned with operant techniques. They were trained to respond to particular forms and shapes. These stimuli represented enemy terrain, and the pigeons were connected in such a way as to be the guidance system for bombs. Whenever the bombs were dropped from airplanes, the pigeons' pecking responses to changes in the shape of the ground would guide the bombs to predetermined targets. Several birds were trained in this procedure, but they were never used for the purposes intended. Fears of public ridicule probably kept the military from actually using these pigeon-guided missiles.

The pigeons were kept isolated for several years until someone decided to conduct an experiment to determine the effects of the previous training on the pigeons' performance. Everyone was amazed when the pigeons performed exactly as they had been taught years before. Even though there was no training for many years, the birds performed flawlessly.

Many psychologists believe that learning is permanent. Several years ago Wilder Penfield demonstrated the possibility of memory being permanent. During an operation on a human brain, he stimulated a portion of it with electrodes. The patient was under local anesthesia and was able to report on the effects of the stimulation. The patient reported that he could remember in acute detail "forgotten" scenes. At a conscious level the patient could not remember the events until he was electrically stimulated. This finding led Penfield to hypothesize that nothing is ever forgotten; things are just misplaced or hidden in the mind.

Human behavior can be permanently changed with the use of behavior modifying techniques. There is a need in mental institutions to reduce the time spent on any one patient so that the nurses can be freed to attend to everyone. It has been found that once the proper operant conditioning had been established, the changes in the patients' behavior continued without the nurses having to monitor them continually.

Another example of the permanency of operant-conditioning

techniques can be seen in the treatment of an anorexic patient by Bachrach in 1965.[1] The patient had *anorexia nervosa* (a chronic failure to eat). At the start of the operant-conditioning program, the patient was five feet, four inches tall and weighed only forty-seven pounds. According to the physicians, she looked like a poorly preserved Egyptian mummy. The patient had been hospitalized eight times before for the same problem. Eating behavior was initiated in the subject simply by reinforcing activities such as lifting food toward her mouth, chewing, and so forth. She was not punished for her noneating, but was given additional rewards for eating. As she ate more and gained weight, other positive reinforcers were given to her. (These additional rewards were directly related to eating behavior.) Shortly after leaving the hospital, the patient was able to enter a business school and broadened her social sphere

With a few simple instructions to the patient and her family, behavioral controls were maintained without costly and constant professional guidance. The conditioning of eating took only a couple of months, but the effects of the techniques lasted for years. The treatment of the case of *anorexia nervosa* involved teaching the patient the elements of self-control so that when she was released she could monitor and maintain her eating behavior. Without the principles of self-control, the effects would have been only temporary. New controls replaced the hospital controls, and these new procedures will last a lifetime because they rely on the individual to continue them. These principles of self-control are the same ones that will make a lasting improvement in you.

Numerous experiments have shown that a person who is instructed in self-control can maintain his behavior without constant professional controls. Once you start practicing the simple self-control principles and techniques, you will have a lifelong improvement program.

THE POWER

Behavior-modification techniques that use the tools of operant conditioning have the power to make or break any of your habits. The habits of a lifetime can be broken and permanent positive behaviors can be started, sometimes in as little as a day of conditioning.

The potency of these simple conditioning techniques has been demonstrated in several experimental and clinical cases. In 1949, Fuller[2] used operant techniques on an individual described as a "human vegetable." The patient had been hospitalized all his life—for eighteen years. He was completely unable to take care of himself. He lay on a bed without moving. He had to be fed, and he could not move. There were huge sores on the man's body due to his immobility. The history of the patient revealed that there had been several attempts to bring the man out of his withdrawn state. These attempts included drugs, water treatments, electroshock therapy, and several other useless procedures. If anything, the treatments tended to push the individual deeper into his isolated condition. After trying for a couple of years, mainly as experiments, the physicians gave up, and the patient was placed in a back ward of the hospital. He was left there for ten or more years before operant-conditioning techniques were used on him.

After the years of being forgotten, the patient was "discovered" by a group of psychologists who felt that they could reach the individual with positive reinforcements. In fact they were right in their guess that the man could be taught with rewards. With the simple drink of the reinforcer of a sugar and milk solution, a completely non-responsive individual was shaped into making several responses.

This is an example of the power of simple operant techniques to modify behavior. If behavior modification could improve this individual, who was inactive for eighteen years, it can help you control yourself.

Excessive Control?

Since the operant-conditioning techniques are so powerful, should you attempt to use them on yourself? Could you become unable to resist the power of the self-induced behavior control program? Could you create a monster in yourself that you could not control? These questions are being debated today by many who feel that the principles of behavior modification are dangerous to use.

Animals have been conditioned to emit 120,000 responses for a reward. What would happen to us if we established such a large requirement for ourselves? Animals in experimental studies have been placed on such strenuous operant programs that they made continual responses until they literally fell over from exhaustion. Some have even died from over-responding. Remember, the experimenters used positive reinforcements, not punishments on the animals.

You may feel concerned that you might end up overworking yourself. There is little to fear about excessive controls in a self-control program. In the previous examples, the experimeter externally manipulated the responding of the animals. With self-control, you are in control of the situation at all times. You can stop at any time you feel oppressed.

The requirement of a hundred thousand responses for a reward does not seem to be detrimental to humans. A writer spends long hours writing down tens of thousands of words before his book can be published and he receives the royalties.

Will operant conditioning cause us to become automatons? Will we become machines that merely respond to the presentation of some stimulus? Since we are establishing the controls in a self-control program, we will not likely establish procedures that will harm us. We are the controllers of ourselves. The power to change our actions lies within us, not outside with someone else.

Recently the use of operant-conditioning techniques in behavior modification programs has met with much criticism. Some courts have ruled that their use in prisons abridges the rights of the inmates, and therefore that they are not to be used in those institutions regardless of their effectiveness to control behavior. Behavior modification of public school children antagonizes many parents who have been successful in removing behavior modification programs from the schools.

Behavior modification is seen as robbing us of our freedom to make independent decisions and our dignity to be human. The purpose of this book is not to add to the debate concerning the evils of human control. The principles of operant conditioning can be used to develop your own personal self-control program. There is no need to have another to control you. The procedures work on rats, pigeons, dogs, alcoholics, and politicians, and they will work for you.

I believe that people should decide for themselves whether or not to apply operant conditioning to change their behavior. The question of who will control is academic when it comes to your wanting to improve yourself. You owe it to yourself to consider behavior modification as an effective and proven method for acquiring self-control. There is nothing in the techniques to fear, especially in terms of self-control.

One of the principles of behavior modification is that to control behavior one should arrange the environment so that the desired behavior is more likely to result. For example, if you want to alter your behavior so that you will awaken at a specified time in the morning, you set an alarm clock. This is a form of stimulus control. When the alarm goes off, you may feel compelled to get up, but you still have the complete ability to disregard it and go back to sleep. The same idea of your being in charge is fundamental to this self-control program.

You can devise a work schedule that makes you feel like attaining some objective. Working toward this goal may require the expenditure of some effort and maybe a little less play than normal; but, you set the goal and the objective for your self-improvement program, and you determine whether you are working too hard.

There may be some justification for fearing a control program that is presided over by another individual, but the self-control program described here is independent of outside controllers. You determine the rewards, and you determine the punishments. You are the controller of this program, and this makes it the best self-control program for *you*.

3

Why change?

Accidents do not follow a normal distribution. A large number of people have no accidents at all. Other people have more than their fair share. Those who have an attitude that they are accident-prone usually are. A person's attitudes have a way of controlling behavior. When we have a positive attitude toward ourselves and to the world around us, we are likely to have a more enjoyable life.

Your attitudes shape the way you see the world. Whether a bricklayer perceives his job as "just laying some bricks," "putting in a long eight hours," or "helping to build a great church" tells a lot about that person's attitude toward his work.

An attitude is an internal state that is not directly observable. We can only infer the qualities of someone else's attitudes. A strict behavioral psychologist is concerned with only those things that he can directly observe. Attitudes are not observable and thus are termed hypothetical constructs; but, we are not concerned with someone else's theory about the existence of our attitudes. We know that we like some things and some people while we have definite dislikes in other matters. Just because we cannot weigh our attitudes does not mean that they do not exist. If we feel them, they exist.

16 Why change?

Your success with any self-improvement program depends entirely upon your attitude and on your beliefs about the efficaciousness of the procedures. If you do have faith in the self-improvement program, then there is a much better chance that you will derive some benefits from it. If you have a negative attitude toward self-improvement programs, then you may have a most difficult time in using any self-improvement plan. If you will just try a couple of the behavior-modification techniques on yourself, you will see that they do work rather well and this should convince you to try others.

MOTIVATION

For a self-control program to work, you must have an answer for a question like the following: "Why do I want to change myself?" If you do not have an answer or if you do not want to change yourself, you will never alter your behavior. Self-change involves motivation, or a reason, for that change.

Can a completely lazy person be changed and motivated to become something more than what he is now? Self-change desires come from within the individual. Force, threats, and coercion are poor ways to control another person's behavior. Once you have taken away the threatening situation, the person reverts to his previous ways of behaving. Unless you can change his attitudes you cannot maintain behavior changed by force. External motivations are effective only as long as they are being applied. Motivation for accomplishing something must be self-generated.

Motivation is a process. The application of operant-conditioning techniques can motivate your behavior for short periods of time until your behavioral changes become substaining in themselves. The proper environment will encourage you to improve. Reinforcements will give temporary boosts to your performances. It just is not possible for others to tell you that you will become motivated. They can describe the various circumstance in which they became motivated to do what they have done. Some can tell you how they became happy with what they do. No one can motivate you if you do not want to be motivated. The techniques are available only to those who *want* to use them.

Your personality represents the complete you that interacts with others in society. It is that aspect of a human being that represents an unique individual. Personality is a composite of previous learning experiences, socialization processes, interactions with others, attitudes, motivations, and so on. Behavior modification can bring about subtle changes in your personality. It may take a long period of time compared with the alterations in some of your other behaviors, but personality can be changed. Changing one's personality requires changing friends, jobs, environments, occupations, play, and attitudes.

Changing one's attitudes may not be a bad idea in some cases, but to change one's personality is a more serious undertaking. It may not be the best solution to your perceived problems. People are always a little dissatisfied with their station in life. A police officer may feel unrewarded in the lack of recognition that he receives from his job. No one seems to care that he risks his life every day. The cop may wish that he was a fire fighter. He thinks that fire fighters have a great life—they have excitement and recognition for their work. Fire fighters may actually desire something besides the long boring hours and the risks. They would gladly trade their jobs to own a business of their own. They see the life of an entrepreneur as one in which the individual is rewarded for his ability to make the right decisions. The business owner has worries, ulcers, and numerous bills. The entrepreneur wishes that he were a college teacher. The college teacher is bored and wants to be a cop. Each person desires something that he is not. People's temperaments may not be suited for what they are doing, and they desire a change. Most everyone has a desire to change, but fear seems to stop people from starting to do what they want to do.

No one wants to spend the rest of his life tightening bolts numbered thirty-six through fifty-one of some product on an assembly line; but, many people do it year after year. It may be their fear of a new job that keeps them where they are. To me it would be a much worse fate to know that next year I will be doing the exact same thing that I am doing today.

If you want to change, then by all means do those things

that will bring about the desired changes. Go to night school, take a correspondence course, meet new people, get out of the rut that you have been in, plan for your future, decide on some definite goals and objectives, and begin now to use the principles and techniques in this book to help improve yourself.

Attitudes and motivation go together to affect your personality and the ways that you think about and perceive the world around you. Negative feelings seem to overshadow and drive out the positive attitudes of individuals. Conscious efforts to be happy and positive toward life will do much to improve the social interactions that you have with others. Just as positive attitudes will help to motivate you, a sour disposition will reinforce negative attitudes and stifle your self-improvement program.

Try a simple experiment. Start off a day with a conscious effort to be rude and curt to everyone that you meet. If a neighbor says hello to you, frown and ignore him. Let the people at work know that you do not think too highly of their ideas; put them in their places. You will notice a change in your relationships with these people the next day. Of course, this experiment will not ruin your life, but if you did this for long you would have few friends. You can easily make a habit out of being unhappy and you will have few friends. You probably do not even have to try this experiment to know what the results are likely to be. A well-meaning apology and an explanation for your behavior will probably patch up hurt feelings. You can see that continual negative attitudes toward those around you will result in a hostile environment. An unhappy and bitter person is more likely to find problems in his life than an individual who is cheerful and positive about the world. Whenever you smile and display a friendly disposition, you are likely to be met with friendly reactions. Hostile behavior causes negative reactions in others, which in turn reinforces our hostility.

PROCRASTINATION

If your self-control program is ever to work for your self-improvement, you must start it. Self-improvement does not come to those who wait for the proper mood to strike. It is easier to find reasons to stall than it is to begin to work. Procrastination has immediate rewards associated with it, while a program of work has few immediate benefits. An improved self is seen as a long way off with a lot of hard work between now and then. With a self-improvement program we can visualize the long-term benefits from using such a program, but they are just too far away to influence our decision to begin to change ourselves.

The only way to start a self-improvement program is to pick a specific time and begin to work on changing yourself at that time. Unless you specifically set a starting time, you are likely to let things slip by and you will never get started.

You should commit yourself to a self-control program by letting others know that you are going to change your life. It is especially effective to tell someone that you do not like. Failure to live up to your commitments will be harder to take, especially if you have told an antagonist.

A contract with yourself is an effective way of getting yourself to adhere to some starting time. Write out the contract, sign it, and honor it. If you cheat on this contract, you will be cheating yourself. Your contract may look something like the following:

> I, _____, will start my self-control program immediately after I have finished reading this book, *Control Yourself*, or at 8 A.M. of the following day. I will not try something too difficult, but I will pick an easy behavior that needs to be changed. I will make an honest and determined effort to follow the principles and techniques of self-control. And I will succeed.

Signed	Date

Keep this self-contract where you will be constantly reminded of your obligation to yourself.

Putting off things until another time is a common problem. There are always seemingly good reasons for not doing something now. Maybe your mood is not quite right, or you feel a cold coming on, or you need a fresh ribbon for the typewriter, or maybe you should drop by and see your friend Charlie. These are just some of the reasons that you can find for not beginning your self-improvement program.

Even business decisions are sometimes hampered by procrastination. If you wanted to, you could spend months researching the alternatives presented by any business decision. Usually the best approach to making a business decision is to pick an alternative and start implementing it at once.

Problem solving, gathering facts, procrastination, and other stalling tactics keep us from taking advantage of life's opportunities. If you desire to improve yourself, or succeed at something, or stop a bad habit, you must make a decision to do it, and more importantly you must start to do it. There is never a better time to improve yourself than right now. Success and fulfillment in a self-improvement program only require you to initiate action.

Do not worry about explaining and defending your actions to others. Your personal improvement is of concern only to you. If you want to practice self-control, then do it. Do not let the attitudes of someone else influence your desire to improve yourself. Many people laughed at the developers of trains and airplanes, but the inventors went ahead with their ideas. Improvement in one's self comes from direct action, not from procrastination.

Being overly-prepared is a common stalling tactic. Any subject can be researched for a great deal of time without any real progress being made toward writing it out. A person went to the library to find some information on immigration into the United States. He only wanted to find the number of individuals by country that came to live in America. The person got interested in finding out about the number of emigrants from the United States during a ten-year period. Then he got sidetracked into finding out which countries they emigrated to and what their occupations were. Some emigrants became meteorologists in Brazil. By closing time, the individual knew a little about Brazil's climate and weather patterns, but he did not know any more about the number of new citizens than when he entered the library six hours before. Procrastination may lead to pleasurable afternoons in the library, but it does not help you to gather the necessary facts.

Another excuse for not beginning or sticking to a plan is the feeling of "I've had a hard day. I think that I'll watch some TV and relax for awhile." A little TV turns into four or five hours and time for bed. You can postpone the painting of the house until winter sets in or until you sell the house. You can stall your self-improvement program until it is too late.

What I have presented here are examples of procrastination. In slightly different ways we are all guilty of putting things off. The determination that you must make with complete honesty to yourself is whether or not you are making the best use of your time. You do not have to drive yourself for eighteen hours a day in order to feel that you are using your time in the best manner. Rest, periods of reflection, daydreaming, and hobbies are also necessary to maintain one's physical and mental health. If you feel that you are spending too much time with nonessential activities, then it is time that you begin to change your behaviors. You must make the decision to control yourself.

If you find that you are having trouble getting started on the following self-controls, and you find yourself wasting precious time with various nonproductive things, you might find a simple rearrangement helpful. Instead of putting your desired self-changes after you have watched television, put them first. Spend ten minutes doing the exercises, or the writing, or whatever. Then watch television, or go to the movies. Do your self-control program first, and follow it with the rewarding activity.

SUMMARY

You are the best judge of what you need.

Do not procrastinate; self-improvement comes only from active doing.

Your attitudes control your behavior, and you can control your attitudes.

4

The principles of self-control

The following principles have been adapted from clinical and experimental situations, the techniques have been shown to work across a wide range of human behaviors. The techniques are not restricted to clinical situations, nor do they demand professional supervision. In fact, many of the techniques of behavior modification were developed for the purpose of allowing individuals to use them in programs of their own self-control. Several important self-control principles will be presented in this chapter. In the next two chapters, the principles of environmental controls and reinforcements will be presented separately because of their great importance in programs of self-control.

The various techniques contained in this self-control program will allow you to engineer self-sustaining behavioral changes in yourself. The principles and techniques are simple to understand and easy to apply. The aim has been to develop a behavior modification program with those principles that are most effective in bringing about lasting self-improvement. Anyone can use this self-control program without costly professional assistance to modify his own behavior quickly and permanently. You determine and control the behavior.

What to Control?

You must determine precisely what behavior you want to change, and how you will measure those changes. According to behavioral psychologists, only measurable and observable behaviors can be modified. Internal processes do not lend themselves to operant controls. These psychologists operate in clinical situations where they do not have time to theorize about some internal factors. They want immediate changes in behaviors of patients that they can see. The psychologists do not delve into underlying mentalistic processes because they are interested in changing overt responses. They feel that if they can keep a patient from beating himself against a wall, then internal states will take care of themselves.

To learn self-control in the easiest manner possible, you should modify behaviors at first. It is much easier to start with overt behaviors and move to mental processes after you have mastered the first stages of self-control. Thought processes are not understood, and the teaching of mental concepts operates mostly on a hit-or-miss basis.

Behaviors are easier to recognize as they occur. Thoughts, emotions, feelings, and other mental activities are difficult to recognize. To begin your self-control program, ask yourself: "If someone else were to control this particular aspect of my behavior, would he be able to record it without having to ask me if I have done it?"

If you are attempting to write a book, approach writing as being words on paper, not as some inner force that shows itself as a finished masterpiece of a story. Change those behaviors that you know how to count, that you can be sure have occurred, and that someone else can also be aware of. Sure, a novel is more than just a certain number of words on paper, but it is easier to control writing activity when you know that you are making progress whenever you write a thousand words a day. Performance must be something that can be objectively measured.

As you develop the necessary skills of self-control, then you can shift from modifying behaviors that are observable to changing and improving activities such as: thinking, memory, emotional control, psychosomatic problems, and creativity. These topics will be explored later in this book.

How to Recognize a Behavior

/ Behavioral changes should start with those responses that are overt and recordable—meaning that someone else can witness the fact. Smoking a cigarette, drinking a glass of water, writing fifty words on a piece of paper, doing four push-ups, and reading a page in a book are activities which can be counted and recorded by you and by anyone else that happens to be watching. These are examples of overt behavior. Staring out a window may be thinking to you, but to someone that is watching you it is an act of staring out the window. The other person has no way of knowing what is going on in your head.

You start with the modification of behavior in order to make thought control at a later time easier to acquire. If you want to decrease the amount of time you spend watching television, you must know first how many hours a day and a week you spend with the television set turned on. It seems likely that as long as the set is on you will probably be watching it. Few people can ignore an operating television set. If the set is on from 6 P.M. to 1 A.M., you are watching from four to six hours of television a night. Part of the time that it is on you may be in the bathroom or the kitchen. That is why I have used the lower figure of four hours. To modify the number of hours that you spend watching the set you should determine the average number of hours that the set is on and then do those things that will lead you to watching it less.

First, reduce the hours of a day that the set is on. Watch only one of your favorite programs a night. Buy an electric timer that allows you to set a specific number of television hours. Then lock up the device so that you cannot change the setting. Find something else to do at night. Move the stimulus (the television) to a part of the house that is not conducive to television watching. Put it in a cold basement or a stuffy attic. This makes television watching less desirable. But the point is, once you have decided upon a behavior that needs to be altered, you have a good starting point for increasing or decreasing the number of occurrences. The recognition of a behavior is the starting point for a successful self-control program. Finding the right behavior to alter is the most difficult part of a self-control program, even more so when you set forth to change the way you think and create. Deciding on a behavior involves the assessment of the impact of altering one behavior on others. What happens when you reduce the number of cigarettes that you smoke a day? Will nail-biting and weight gain be the result? Maybe the behavior that you need to change is keeping your hands busy, not just the reduction of a smoking behavior.

Sometimes the end goal of your self-control program may be the acquisition of more than one behavior. A singer must understand music, know the scales, and have physical control of his breathing. A painter must know something about paints, canvas, brush strokes, and perspectives. The attainment of a final goal may involve several behaviors along the way.

Are You Getting Better?

In the 1920s, Emil Coué issued his famous statement for the achievement of self-mastery. He wrote: "Every day, in every way, I am getting better and better."[1] His belief was that self-improvement came from repeating this phrase several times a day. Through repetition, the subconscious was supposed to acquire positive feelings.

The difficulty in applying Coué's autosuggestion edict effectively is that there is no objective way to measure your improvements. You never know for sure if you are actually getting any better. Self-control programs must be formulated on the use of specific, concrete, and explicit guidelines. Objective measurements should be used.

Every day you could repeat the following slogan to yourself: "Every day, I am becoming a greater and greater painter." You are not likely to become any more proficient at the art of painting unless you actually spend a little time each day in studying and practicing the craft. Once you have entered into an art program, you can actually see your improvements. You do not have that opportunity when you try to talk to your subconscious. Skills come from active practice that serves as an objective measurement of your performance changes.

A record of the average number of responses you make at the start of a self-control program should be made. This average number of times that you have engaged in the act during a day is called a base line, or an operant level, by operant psychologists.

The base line is used to measure the amount of changes that have been brought about by the self-control program. To reduce the number of cigarettes smoked during a day, you need some idea how many you normally smoke. It is easier to see the benefits of behavior control when the daily responses are compared with the start of the program. If your behavior is improving, the knowledge of this reinforces your future behaviors. If your actions are getting worse (you are smoking more than the average number represented by the base line), negative sanctions may be applied so that you will put in more effort to control your behavior.

If you desire to spend more time engaged in some activity, you need to know how much time you normally spend doing it. The base line of that behavior gives you a starting point. If you find that you average about ten minutes a day studying, you can use this as the operant level for studying behavior. Tomorrow you can spend eleven minutes doing nothing but studying, which is definitely an improvement over the average time. By gradually increasing the time spent each day in that activity you can improve your performance. The base line serves to tell you if you are getting better or worse.

The Contract

Once you have decided upon the behavior to be controlled, and you have established the method for measuring that behavioral change, you can establish the final goal or objective of this particular self-control. The most effective way to work toward some goal is to make that goal precise and objective. Then you will know when you reach it. The best way to make a goal precise is to write it down.

To reinforce your desires to attain some final thing, it is helpful to make a contract with yourself. This contract should specify what the final goal is to be, any intermittent stops along the way to the attainment of that goal, the necessary behaviors, the way that your behaviors are to be measured and rewarded, and the penalties that are to be given if the behavioral standards are not met. Picture this instrument as being a binding contract with yourself. It is your agreement with yourself that maintains your compliance.

A personal contract that is written to yourself will help to enforce your decisions. Numerous studies have shown the effectiveness of these self-contracts in altering and controlling behaviors. Subjects who have voluntarily entered into written agreements to follow certain courses of action have followed the self-control programs. Deviations from the contract were met with negative self-coercions that channeled the subjects' behaviors toward the goal. Maintenance of the behavior was done by the subjects without pressures from any outside forces. The commitments that the individuals made to themselves caused their adherence to the self-improvement programs. Threats, punishments, constraints, or other external ploys were not necessary to get the individuals to behave properly.

I have a bad habit of putting things off. I was called upon to deliver a short, twenty-minute speech on the commodity futures market. Previous experience had taught me that I would not prepare a talk until it was almost time to deliver the speech. Sometimes I would wait until a couple of hours before the scheduled time of the speech to decide upon what to say.

I developed a program to help me prepare this speech in advance of the scheduled date. My main concern was not to prepare the greatest speech, even though I hoped that it would be good, but to gather the necessary information and write out enough words on the topic to get me through a twenty-minute talk. This was my intended goal—to have enough words to say to fill out a specific time span.

To set the goal objectively, I needed to know approximately how many words a minute I could speak in a normal manner. I determined this quite easily by reading a newspaper out loud as if I were giving it as a speech, timing myself for a minute, and counting the number of words that I was able to speak during that minute. I found that I should be able to say about 2,500 words in twenty minutes. This is about ten pages of writing.

The first part of my speech preparation was to research the topic. I decided to spread out this task over the period of a week, instead of doing it all in one day. Also, the writing of the speech was to be spread over several days.

I decided to spend thirty minutes a day for five days researching the commodity futures market. After the period of research, I would spend two days just thinking about what I had read. I felt that fifteen minutes just before bed would be ample time to think about the subject. I allowed myself a half an hour for six days to write the speech out. The amount of time I scheduled myself to spend in preparing the twenty minute speech was six hours.

I felt that I needed this much time to prepare for such a short speech for two reasons: (1) the impact of the speech had to be good, and (2) I wanted to know the subject area well enough to be able to answer questions at the end of my talk.

The following is the contract that I developed for myself:

I, David R. Wheeler, on this day of August 28, 1975 do hereby enter into this agreement with myself. I will observe the following schedule for the preparation of my twenty (20) minute speech to be delivered on September 11, 1975. For the next five days I shall gather information on the topic of my speech entitled: "The Commodity Futures Market for Fun and Profit." The amount of time I shall spend in research each of these five days will be no more than thirty minutes, or a total of two and one-half hours. The next two days I shall spend fifteen minutes just before going to sleep thinking about the topic and the research. Following that, I shall spend thirty minutes a day for six days writing the speech. When I have put in the required number of minutes in any day, I shall immediately quit even though I may not be finished with whatever I am working on at the moment.

When I have completed the speech, I shall give myself a good meal and treat myself to a movie or play. If I do not spend the required number of minutes on the assigned task during any of the days, I shall not watch television that night.

Signed this day of August 28, 1975

This contract with myself was effective in getting me to adhere to a specific plan. I decided upon the goal, selected the behaviors that would lead to the attainment of that objective, and planned for daily increments of speech preparation. I included both rewards and punishments to motivate my behavior toward my desired goal. I signed the contract, which indicated to me my intent to honor the terms of the agreement. If I broke a rule as outlined in the contract, it would be tantamount to breaking my word.

The written contract reinforces your intent to follow a specific plan to obtain a goal. I did not tell myself that I was going to write the Great Speech. I am not sure what that means, nor even how to measure it. I did know that if I were to spend enough time preparing for that speech I would do a better job on it than if I were to toss it together an hour before time to give it. All I did was to arrange the expenditure of time so that I was assured of enough words to say.

Your personal contract can be as brief as you want. The power of the contract to modify and maintain your behavior is a device that can be used to advantage with any number of your behaviors.

Shaping

Shaping a behavior means that you reinforce small units that approximate the final desired goal. If you are writing a book of 100,000 words, you would most likely want to break this task into smaller units. These segments could be a certain number of words or various lengths of time. Few, if any, could sit down and write 100,000 words at one time. But by writing an hour or two a day, one could ultimately reach that objective. Shaping writing behavior would mean that you would work for a while, take a break or a reward, then return at a later time to resume writing. This you would keep up until you finished that task. Rewards may be a glass of water after every twenty-minute writing effort.

The right behaviors must be shaped by the giving of reinforcements after the completion of each of the behaviors. Behaviors should be rewarded frequently and immediately. If you want to be able to speak in front of groups of people, you must reinforce your behavioral acts that lead up to a speech. This may be approached by practicing the talk in front of one or two close friends, then you could give the speech in front of a larger group, and maybe you could find three or four individuals that are strangers to you and present your speech to them. Shaping the speech behavior comes about from the reinforcement of larger and larger units of behaviors that approximate the final goal. The same procedure works for the learning of painting, singing, or driving a race car.

To shape a behavior you must start with a small part of the final behavior. You gradually lengthen the time spent doing that behavior, or you increase the size of the behavior. Shaping is successful because you reward yourself for each unit of behavior or each unit of time instead of punishing yourself by feeling guilty for not doing something.

Shaping can bring about dramatic results. Two catatonic schizophrenics who had not talked for nineteen and fourteen years were shaped with the use of rewards into talking.[2] The reward was chewing gum. The experimenters selected a response of eye movement (it was one of the few behaviors emitted by one of the subjects) to reward. For a couple of weeks, the subject was given the gum whenever he turned his eyes to look at it. After that conditioning had taken place, the experimenters started to reinforce the movement of the subject's lips. Next, the experimenters said: "Say 'gum.'" They would reward any vocalizations that came close to sounding like "gum." Within two months (eighteen teaching sessions) the patients could talk. Talking behavior was shaped with rewards.

To shape your own behavior, you must not reward yourself too frequently or the reinforcements will lose their motivating power. Reward your behavior often but with small amounts of reinforcements. Also, do not require too much work for too little reward. If you expect too much from yourself, you are likely to be frustrated.

CONSISTENT EFFORTS

↘ Self-improvement requires a daily effort. It may mean only ten minutes a day, but it should be done every day. If you have decided that it will take a certain number of minutes or hours to accomplish your goals, and you have devised a plan that includes a regular schedule of responses, you must adhere to the program. If you skip a day you are cheating yourself.

↳ Consistency means that you constantly meet the requirements of the self-control program. Haphazard attempts in self-control will bring about a deterioration in your ability to control yourself.

↳ Do not set your daily standards for expected performance so high that you can never hope to attain them. If you find yourself unable to meet your expectations, rearrange your proposed schedule so that behavioral attainment is possible without unwarranted pressure and stress. It is better to have a twenty minute a day self-improvement program than it is to expect yourself to spend an impossible twelve hours a day improving yourself.

The beneficial self-control program is the one that you practice religiously, at scheduled times, and you engage in without interruptions. The units of work should be modest and realistic.

You must be honest to yourself. If you have decided to spend every other day doing exercises for five minutes, you should not rationalize your way out of doing them one day. What do you think of a friend who does not stand by his word to you? Or what do you think about those people who always have a ready excuse for not improving their lives? ("I'm too tired to go to night school, especially after I have worked for eight hours.") And finally, how do you feel about those people who say that they really ought to do that, but never seem to get around to doing it? Exchange "you" for the other people in the following questions and ask yourself this: "How will I feel about myself when I do not honor my own self-improvement contract?" Devise a program that is attainable. Stick to the schedule. Be consistent. And you will control yourself.

Gradual Changes

Learning is an incremental process. It takes time and practice to become good at anything. Each day you should become a little better at self-control than the day before. The principle of gradually changing your behavior will work whether you desire to increase some behavior (i.e., reading, studying, or exercises) or to decrease some behavior (i.e., smoking, drinking, or daydreaming).

Suppose that you want to get yourself into better physical shape. You decide that your end goal will be to do 100 sit-ups (along with some other exercises to balance out the exercise program), and to lose twenty-five pounds in the process. You know that there are two ways of reaching both these objectives. One way is to work the weight off by doing more physical activities. The second way of reducing your weight is to cut down on calories. Working out a program for self-control will allow you to build up your body and to reduce your weight at the same time.

The number of exercises should be increased each day. Weight loss should be gradual. This can be accomplished by a self-control program. You can put yourself under a time limit. Each day you spend ten minutes doing exercises. After you have become accustomed to the physical exertion, you can gradually increase the amount of time that you spend on that activity.

Start with a small amount of time and gradually increase it. Remember, if you do not spend any time now working out, then one minute a day is a big improvement. Another way to begin an exercise program is to do a certain amount of exercises each day. Your base line for this approach may involve running until you feel the first sign of difficulty. Or do as many push-ups as you can until you just begin to get tired. Do not do one more or run another step; just stop. The next day gradually increase the number of feet that you ran from the day before. Or try to do one more push-up than the previous day. The principle that you should follow in self-improvement is to find a comfortable starting point and gradually increase the number of behaviors that you do from there.

Trying to lose twenty-five pounds in a week or attempting 100 sit-ups in the first day will destroy any future desire that you may have to reach those goals. Too much of a required behavioral change will force you out of a self-improvement program quickly.

Decreases or increases in one's behavior must be kept gradual so that mental and physical discomforts will not destroy your self-control. Steady progress must replace crash programs for changing one's life.

Do not get discouraged with the seeming lack of change or improvement. Some habits take a long time to be replaced. Do not expect to change something overnight that you have been doing for years. Behavior-modification techniques have been effective in bringing about swift changes in some instances, while in other clinical situations modifications in behaviors have taken four or five months. If you make a determination that you want to change something, develop a realistic program to obtain that goal, and give the program time to work for you. But once you have made yourself the commitment to change yourself, plan to stick to it. Do not expect a half-hearted self-control program to work.

Charting Your Success

Since you have determined what behavior is to be modified, and you have decided how it is to be measured, you can devise a chart so that you can actually see the changes in your performance. Get some graph paper and label one axis the time span that your self-control program is going to cover. The other axis will be the number of responses that occur. You will start off by determining the average number of operant behaviors (your activities), and should place this base line upon your self-control chart. This is your standard that will tell you if you are getting better or worse.

Each day keep a record of the number of times you engage in the behavior that you are controlling. If it is smoking that you are trying to control, keep a daily record of the cigarettes that you light and smoke. A small plastic counter or a notebook can be used to get an objective record of the smoking behavior. Each day tally the number of cigarettes and graph that number on your smoking chart. Every day you will be able to determine exactly whether or not your smoking behavior is improving.

For many years psychologists have attempted to be more objective in their understanding of human behavior. Some psychologists have denied the existence of any internal states of behavior. Books on self-improvement have suggested that if you wanted to improve yourself, you must reach your subconscious. Charting changes in behaviors is a better method for altering one's self. It is easy to use and not subject to interpretation. A push-up can be seen and counted. Smoking one less cigarette today than you did yesterday is verifiable.

Lines indicating your performance can be reinforcing. To see that week by week you are losing weight gives you a sense of accomplishment. The daily feedback that you get from charting your behaviors protects your self-control program from spasmodic efforts and temporary setbacks. Graphs or charts let you analyze your behavior and control your performance.

SUMMARY

Each of the self-control principles contained in this chapter will allow you to control yourself. They are simple, but they will do an excellent job of modifying or maintaining your behaviors. Take a few minutes each day for two weeks and apply these principles (and the ones in the following chapters of this book) to some habit or problems that you may be having. The principles of behavior modification are too effective not to use for your self-improvement.

Start your self-control program by modifying behaviors.

A behavior is something that can be measured and observed.

Strive for objective measurements of behaviorial changes so that you will know if your performances are improving or getting worse.

A written contract with yourself is effective in keeping you at work on your self-control.

The final behavior or goal that you are striving for in terms of self-control must be attainable.

Gradually shape your behavior toward the goal.

Be consistent in your efforts to gain control of yourself. You cannot improve yourself with half-hearted attempts.

Your daily expectations must not be set too high.

Record the number of times you engage in the behavior during the day and enter this number on a chart or graph.

Charting your behavior has a tendency to reinforce your desires to improve yourself.

5

Positive consequences

Every day your behavior is shaped and controlled by rewards. These rewards may come from external sources. Among such rewards are a paycheck, praise from others, and food. Or rewards may be internally generated as is the case with self-satisfaction, self-praise, or happiness with one's family and friends. In controlling your behavior, you are just as motivated by self-rewards as by the rewards given to you by someone else.

Your behavior can be altered and maintained through self-rewards. There does not have to be an external giver of rewards for you to be able to control yourself. You can arrange your reinforcements just as effectively as an employer can reinforce his employees for their work. A self-monitored program of rewards (or positive reinforcements) can modify your behavior.

In 1967 Albert Bandura and Bernard Perloff tested the effectiveness of self-controlled and externally controlled reinforcement programs.[1] These researchers found that individuals who chose their own performance levels, and rewarded themselves on the attainment of that behavioral level, performed just as well as a group that had its standards set for them and was rewarded by the researchers. The performances of the self-control group and the externally controlled group were significantly better than a third group, which received no rewards at all for the same task. Rewards or reinforcements improved the behavior, regardless of whether the rewards were presented by an authority or were self-determined and self-administered.

You can prescribe to yourself a standard of behavior, measure your own level of compliance, and reward yourself just as effectively as if someone else were controlling you. Evidence from Bandura and Perloff's study, along with other clinical and experimental research, shows that self-reinforced procedures, if implemented correctly, can produce lasting changes in your behavior.

Self-reinforcements work. High levels of performance can be expected even without external controls. Many of the subjects in self-control experiments gave themselves small amounts of rewards for large amounts of work. It seems that in the judgment of the individuals themselves, doing the job is just as important as getting something for doing it.

Rewards and the schedules in which they occur will be a most important aspect of your self-control program. Many remarkable things have been accomplished through the proper use of reinforcements. Pigeons have been taught to play table tennis. Rats have been taught to find their way to pieces of cheese in mazes. Humans have been taught to regain their ability to speak.

Rewards have been used by psychologists to get animals to make tens of thousands of responses in order to receive a drink or piece of food. Patients in hospitals have had their behaviors changed permanently through the application of positive reinforcements.

What Gives Us Pleasure?

What is a reward? What is a positive reinforcer? I have been using these terms to show how behavior can be controlled. We accept the fact that getting rewarded for something is good. We like to do things that give us pleasure. We like to be rewarded. You know what you like and do not like. A piece of moldy cheese is a reinforcer for a hungry rat. Would you work hard for a slice of the same cheese? One person's reward may be another person's dislike. This is not always true, but it happens just often enough to make defining a reward difficult. Also, rewards in some circumstances may become punishments.

Rewards and positive reinforcements have several meanings, depending upon which theoretical school of psychology you happen to read. Behavioral psychologists speak about reinforcers as being those things that change the probability of a response occurring. Thus, getting paid increases the probability that you will work. Getting paid is a reinforcer. In terms of operant conditioning, a positive reinforcer is that event following an emitted behavior that tends to make it more likely for the person to do that behavior again. (Negative reinforcers reduce the probability that the behavior will be done again. This principle will be discussed in the next chapter.)

For self-control the question becomes: "What should I use to reward my behavior so that I will be more likely to do it again next time?" This is an easy question to answer. Anything that gives you pleasure is a reward. If you like to watch television, read, walk, paint, eat, take naps, collect coins, take trips, visit friends, listen to concerts, watch movies, fish, build furniture, or to do any other thing, you have a reinforcer. Anything that makes you feel good can be used to motivate your behavior and to control your future actions.

Rewards may be small but still do a good job in motivating you. A sip of water can be rewarding. You can set up a self-control program that allows for a reinforcement of a cracker and a shot glass of milk every thirty minutes. The simplicity of something like this may be deceiving. Numerous studies have shown that this little technique of giving yourself a little reward every so often is effective in controlling your behavior.

Contingencies

The key to the success of behavior-modification programs is in the concept of contingency management. Contingency theory presents the idea that we are influenced by the resulting consequences of our behaviors. Sticking our hand into a fire influences our future actions.

The threats of punishment and the promises of rewards that are present in our environment shape our behavior. Contingency is the concept that is used to explain why people behave as they do. Contingency management is the managing of those events that are contingent upon the behavior.

If you are going to manage the contingent reinforcements of the environment so that the desired self-controlled behaviors will result, you must answer the following questions:

1. What are your behaviors that you want to increase, decrease, start, or stop?
2. What are the events (contingencies) of your environment that are maintaining your behaviors or your lack of behaviors?
3. What in your environment can you change so that your behavior can be altered?
4. What self-rewards and self-reinforcements will effectively modify your behavior?
5. Which schedule of reinforcement should be used to maintain the new behavior?

To develop self-control you must select those things that you find rewarding and make them contingent upon the occurrence of the desired behavior. For example, if you find it difficult to study for that correspondence course, decide upon a small unit of time that you can spend on it each day. Ten to fifteen minutes a day may be the ideal amount of time to start with. Write out your contract to oblige you to that amount of study time. Do nothing but study the correspondence course material for the agreed-to time each day. Then schedule your contingency reinforcements. You will allow yourself to watch television, go to that movie, or visit a friend *after* you have studied for fifteen minutes. This is what contingency management is—the arrangement of the environmental elements (in this case, rewards) to control one's behavior. You do not get to have any of your normal rewards until you have performed a small amount of studying.

Studying for just fifteen minutes a day is a good way to get into a daily study habit, but when it is necessary to spend significantly more time on a project than fifteen minutes a day, you must develop intermediate reinforcements along the way. How to schedule these rewards will be discussed shortly.

WHEN TO GIVE

The future of your modified behavior depends upon when you schedule the rewards. Not only are desired behaviors shaped with reinforcements, but also their resistance to change is a function of the schedule used to reward those behaviors. You can establish various standards of performance that will be rewarded according to a half dozen different programs. When to reward your self-control behavior is an important consideration because different schedules give different results.

Trying to establish those behaviors necessary to reach a complex and distant goal requires the use of rewards at various behavioral points along the way. A college education takes about four years. The goal at the end of those long years is a degree that entitles the possessor to a better job with greater satisfaction than his present work. Without some kind of rewards along the way, a long-range reward may lose its motivating strength. If this happens, you could become a self-control "drop-out." Schedule your rewards as you make progress toward an objective, as well as arranging those reinforcements at the end of the program that are contingent upon the required behaviors.

There are several reinforcing events during the career of a college student. Grades are rewarding because knowledge of one's performance level is reinforcing. Social activities help to maintain the behavior of going to school.

You can reward every behavior that you do as part of your self-control program. Continual and immediate reinforcement is highly recommended whenever you are acquiring a new behavior. The fastest way to learn something is to do it and get a reinforcement. If we have been rewarded every time that we did something, we would get discouraged quickly when those rewards were stopped completely. Our tolerance for frustration is low under continual reinforcement schedules. Reinforcing yourself constantly is not the best method to maintain behaviors over long periods of time and where conditions will not allow such frequent rewards.

Once you have learned a new task, you should switch to an intermittent schedule of reinforcement. This is the idea of giving yourself rewards occasionally for the desired behaviors. Every response is not met with a reward under an intermittent reward schedule. You can establish and monitor a self-control schedule under noncontinuous reinforcements once you have the necessary experience and skill under continuous reinforcements.

Intermittent schedules have been divided into two categories, depending on whether responses or the passage of time is used as the basis for reinforcements. Either category can be rewarded according to some set number or variable number of occurrences.

Interval Schedules of Reinforcement

After the passage of an interval of time, and contingent upon the performance of the desired self-improvement behavior, you can give yourself a reward.

A. Fixed interval schedules of reinforcements occur at the end of specific lengths of time. The interval of time is constant. Receiving a paycheck at the end of a week of work is an example of a fixed interval reinforcement program. An operant behavior that corresponds to this kind of schedule is the increases in activity associated with looking for the mail carrier to arrive at a specific time.

Fixed intervals generate minimum efforts. When the reinforcements are withdrawn, the behaviors gradually taper off.

To put yourself on a fixed interval schedule, arrange for reinforcement breaks at the end of every twenty minutes or half-hour of activity. You can experiment with different lengths of time to find the one best suited to your needs. At the start of your self-control program, determine how long it will take to accomplish the task. Divide this total amount of time into smaller units and arrange for rewards to follow each of the sub-units of time.

Reinforcing your behavior under this schedule will gradually bring you nearer your goal.

B. Variable interval schedules of reinforcements are contingent upon the performance of the behavior and occur at the end of time periods that vary in length. Once again the rates of the behaviors are lower than those conditioned under ratio schedules, but long sustained responding is the result. When the reinforcements are withdrawn, the behaviors gradually taper off.

There are several methods to set up a variable interval schedule for self-control. You could throw some dice and use the numbers on them as the number of minutes that you must work on a task before receiving your reinforcement. Or you can draw cards from a deck and use the numbers on them to give you the time interval. (The face cards could count as ten minutes.)

Even though it is the interval of time that must pass before rewards are given, you should remember that the rewards are still contingent upon the occurrence of the behaviors. Do not take a nap for ten minutes and expect to reward yourself. Reinforcements are given whenever the desired self-control behaviors have been done.

Whenever you are devising your variable interval schedule, remember that the time interval varies for each sequence. One set of behaviors may have to occur for five minutes before being rewarded. During the next interval it may be fifteen minutes before a reinforcement is given. The intervals that you select should be positioned around the best time interval for you. For example, if you find that you work well for thirty minutes at a time, you should structure your variable intervals to average thirty minutes.

Response Schedules of Reinforcement

When reinforcements are based on some number of responses, the reward program is termed a ratio or response schedule. Response schedules are effective in getting someone to perform a great amount of responses to get a reward. Writers put 100,000 words onto paper before they get their rewards. The pay writers get for their efforts is contingent upon their completion of a manuscript. Any work in which the pay follows a completed job is a ratio or response schedule. The faster you do your job, the more rewards you receive.

A. Fixed ratio schedules of reinforcement are arranged so that after every X number of responses a reward is given. The X can be almost any number of responses that can be conditioned. Rates of 100,000 have been achieved after a week of training. This means that the subject would have to make 100,000 responses before a reinforcement is received. Under a fixed response schedule there is a short pause just after the subject receives the reinforcement before he continues his operant behaviors. When the reinforcements are withdrawn, responses continue at a rapid rate for some time, then they stop fairly quickly.

A reading assignment or a term paper of a specific length are examples of fixed response schedules. This is an easy program to develop and use in your self-control. You determine the goals that you want to reach, decide upon the behaviors that will have to be emitted in order to arrive at those objectives, and decide on the number of responses you will make before allowing yourself a reinforcement. Your task may be to read a book during the forthcoming month. Breaking this task into parts, you can decide how many pages a day you should read. Each day when you have finished the required number of pages you give yourself a reinforcement. Any desired response can be rewarded under this schedule. The harder you work the more the rewards you get.

B. Variable response schedules of reinforcement reward performances on a random basis. There is no set number of responses that will result in a reinforcement. Depending upon your self-control purposes, you may reward the twentieth response, the fortieth response, and the eightieth response in a series. Performance under a variable ratio schedule is stable and consistent, and it has a high response rate. This is the most powerful method for controlling behavior. The slot machines in gambling casinos pay off according to a variable ratio schedule. Even when the occasional reinforcements are completely withdrawn, the conditioned behavior is almost impossible to extinguish. You can establish a variable schedule to reward your responses by using dice or cards to establish the required number of behaviors to be emitted before a reward is given. For a self-control program, it would be better to establish the conditioned behavior with either a fixed interval or fixed ratio schedule, and then to change to a variable ratio schedule at a later time.

Combination Reinforcement Schedules

The world we live in rewards us according to all the above schedules. Sometimes we get paid at the end of a fixed interval of time. We have trouble with our cars just after the warranty has expired. Sometimes we get praise for the work that we have done, and sometimes we get criticized.

Studies with animals have shown that multiple schedules of reinforcement lead to more sensitive reactions to stimulation. There were more responses made to a combination of reinforcement schedules than to one type alone.

Change the schedules that you use to reward your performances. Experiment with two or three of the schedules in combination. This will lead to a more interesting self-control program.

SELF-SATISFYING REINFORCEMENTS

Small, intermittent rewards during a self-control program will modify the behavior until your progress becomes personally satisfying enough so that the knowledge that you are improving can in itself be rewarding. It is necessary to arrange for your reinforcers along the way to self-control until you are able to see the new, slim person in the mirror.

When the self-improvement program has been firmly established, certain behaviors will produce feedback concerning your level of performance. Overeating after you have been on a weight control program will cause you to evaluate that behavior and that will produce negative sanctions within you. Your agreements with yourself to follow a certain course of action means that your feelings of right and wrong will keep your deviations from the self-improvement program to a minimum.

Summary

Behavior is shaped and controlled with reinforcements.

Giving rewards to yourself is an effective method for modifying and controlling your own behavior.

There does not have to be an external agent that gives you your rewards.

Anything may act as a reinforcer or reward.

Our behavior is influenced by the consequences of our actions.

To develop a program for your self-improvement, you must determine those things that you like and make them contingent upon the occurrence of the desired response.

Do not give yourself rewards before you have finished doing the behavior.

Different schedules of reinforcements modify behavior differently.

Continuous reinforcement of a behavior reduces the effectiveness of the motivator to control the response.

Fixed interval reward schedules generate minimum efforts.

Variable interval reward schedules cause low but sustained rates of responding.

Fixed ratio schedules of rewards lead to higher responding rates than under the interval schedules.

Variable ratio reward schedules cause the most stable, consistent, and highest rate of responding of any of the various methods of rewarding behavior.

Establish the conditioning under continuous reinforcements and shift to one of the intermittent schedules later on in your self-control program.

Multiple schedules of rewards bring about sensitivity in reacting to stimuli.

6

Negative consequences

The positive ways in which we can control our behaviors were discussed in the previous chapter. These positive procedures are formulated on the principle of behavior modification that when behaviors are immediately followed by positive consequences they will tend to be repeated. In this chapter we will be interested in those methods that can be used to reduce the occurrence of certain behaviors.

Extinction, satiation, aversive stimuli, negative reinforcement, withdrawing positive reinforcements, and punishments are techniques that can be used to reduce unwanted behaviors. Some of the methods are highly controversial. The improper use of some (especially punishment) can be dangerous. Not only will the improper use cause physical damage, but also there may be permanent emotional changes brought about.

Before you start to use punishment or negative reinforcers to control your behaviors, try applying the positive approaches.

Generally we can reduce unwanted responses by two methods. We can remove the positive consequences that maintain the behavior. Stop the positive reinforcements that follow the habitual behavior. The second general procedure for reducing behaviors is to establish aversive contingencies to follow the behavior.

Aversive contingencies are those events of the environment that follow a behavior and tend to reduce its rate of occurrence. When a behavior is followed by some aversive consequences, the behavior is reduced; but once you withdraw the aversive contingencies the behavior reappears. This is another reason to try to establish positive consequences to control your behavior. The effects of punishment, aversive contingencies, and the other behavior-reducing methods are good only as long as you keep following the behavior with them. Establishing positive consequences for your actions may become permanent.

Knowing that if we do something it will be followed by aversive consequences, we will tend to avoid that activity. We behave in certain ways because we know what the effects from that will be. Most people avoid breaking traffic laws because of their fears of the consequences—getting a traffic ticket.

Negative reinforcers cause our compliance in certain ways because we do not want the undesirable stimuli to occur. Negative reinforcers involve the removal of an unwanted event contingent upon certain performance. When noise is made contingent upon a stuttering response, the stuttering decreases. To apply this principle to your self-control program, you could rig a bell to your television. As long as the set remained on, the bell would ring. This procedure will help in reducing the time spent watching television.

Anything that you dislike can be used as a negative reinforcer. You must make an evaluation of your choice of reinforcers. If they are not aversive enough, they will not be effective in controlling your behavior. But, if the punishment is too strong, the chances are good that an emotional reaction will be established. This emotional reaction may generalize to other behaviors and to other situations.

Any of the methods used to extinguish your undesired behavior can take a long time to accomplish what you want, and some result in undesirable reactions. The one rule you should keep in mind as you develop a self-improvement program using any of the techniques in this chapter is: Always give yourself an alternative to the behavior that you are attempting to modify. If you are trying to quit smoking, and you are using a program of aversive consequences, give yourself an alternative. These alternatives will be more effective if they are positively reinforcing. In short, say no to one of your behaviors, but say yes to another behavior to take its place.

Punishment

You may punish yourself for behaving in certain ways by: (1) presenting a negative reinforcer or aversive stimuli whenever that behavior occurs, or (2) denying yourself a positive reward that you would normally expect to receive. With either approach you must arrange the environmental contingencies so that the punishment depends upon the behavior.

Punishment causes emotional reactions. You begin to fear doing things that may be only slightly similar to the behavior that you are trying to stop. Punishment, because of this effect of emotional reaction and generalized negative feelings, is a dangerous method to use on yourself. It is hard to predict the outcomes of using this technique. Its effects depend on emotional stability, motivational factors, schedules of presentation, how long the punishment is delivered, and the availability of alternative courses of action. Punishment seems to work best when it is used along with other techniques. An alternative that can be reinforced should be made available so that when you punish yourself for a behavior you can shift to something else.

Thus, if you rig your cigarette case with an unpleasant aroma that is released each time you open it to get a smoke, you should have another similar box containing something that you like, such as a piece of candy or lollipops. If the aversive stimulus of the bad smell is too bad or too severe, the aversion you develop can spread to the practices of self-control. It might be that if you punish yourself too hard, you will drop out of the self-improvement program. You might throw away the boxes and continue smoking.

A useful technique to punish undesired behaviors or to put more pressure to bear on your voluntary compliance to the self-improvement program has to do with negative aversive stimuli.

50 Negative consequences

An aversive event or stimulus can be anything that you dislike doing. This may be a food that you do not like, a person you do not get along with very well, or an organization whose ideals you disagree with. The stronger the dislike, the more powerful the effects of the aversive stimuli become.

As an example of the use of a negative aversive stimulus in your self-control program, let us imagine that you have a task that you should finish by a certain date. It might take about ten weeks to accomplish the task. Pick an organization that you hate and write out ten checks to this organization. (The amount depends on how aversive you want to make the situation.) If during the ten weeks you do not perform according to your self-contract, mail a check to the organization. If each week you meet the minimum requirements that you have outlined for yourself, you can tear up that week's check. If you are attempting to write a thesis, a dissertation, or a novel, you might schedule yourself to finish a chapter a month. Failure to finish a chapter in a month would mean that you punish yourself with an aversive consequence. You might give away your favorite book or be nice to an enemy.

You must make the aversive event contingent upon your not doing the correct thing. If you behave as you agreed to, then you suffer no bad consequences.

Contractors have to pay penalties when they do not finish their building as they had agreed. This contingency money is forwarded to a third party, who holds it until the construction is finished or pays it to the person that is having the building constructed whenever the schedule is not met. The power of this technique is increased if you get someone to hold the checks for you. If you do not show them the chapter for that month, they are to immediately mail your check to the organization, or they are to give your book to someone. If you meet the terms of the agreement, then they are to give that month's check back to you.

If you are not to feel the effects of the punishment, you must perform the required behaviors. Your agreement to the self-control program is maintained by the threat of aversive consequences.

EXTINCTION

We engage in certain behaviors because we find them rewarding. To control yourself you must arrange the reinforcing events of the environment. To stop a behavior from occurring you must find a way to stop the reinforcing elements from being contingent upon that response. Behavior is extinguished when the rewards that usually follow a response are withdrawn. We just will not do something unless it is in some way rewarding.

Pavlov was able to extinguish behaviors by presenting the conditioned stimulus without the unconditioned stimulus being paired with it. Ringing the bell enough times without the sight of the food led the animal to extinguish his salivation response.

If you can arrange the elements of your environment so that reinforcements do not follow the behavior, that particular response will gradually taper off. The extinguished behavior is not permanently removed. It is only displaced. Extinguished responses easily recover whenever the reinforcing elements start to follow the behavior once again. It is hard to structure environmental elements so that the behaviors are never again rewarded. The most successful approach to controlling behaviors through the removal of reinforcements is done by combining extinction with positive reinforcements of a competing response.

Behavior can be extinguished through an application of symbolically produced consequences. A response is regulated by the use of imagined self-reinforcements. Implosive therapy involves exposing a patient to the most horrible aversive stimuli that can be imagined.[1] The patients are asked to think about the threatening situations over and over again. Implosive therapy is supposed to extinguish the emotional behavior because the continual exposures are repeated without any physical harm. Thinking constantly about living in a cesspool will reduce the fear of dirt on a doorknob.

Implosive therapy could be highly dangerous to experiment with on yourself. The full effects of this technique have not been explored, and it is possible that anxiety can be increased with the improper application of implosive therapy.

SATIATION

Satiation occurs when there is a decrease in the number of your responses due to continual and excessive reinforcement. A continuous reinforcement schedule will produce satiation quicker than an intermittent reinforcement schedule.

Ayllon was able to reduce a patient's responses by allowing the person to engage in the particular activity as often as she wanted.[2] This patient had a habit of hoarding towels in her room. Nurses continually removed the towels from the woman and kept telling her to stop. The behavior had gone on for years before Ayllon set about to correct the situation. The patient was given as many towels as she wanted. No one said anything to her regarding the accumulation of towels that she had in her room. After a week of unrestricted towel collecting the patient suddenly started to remove some of the 600 towels from her room. She took all the towels out and never again hoarded towels.

Generally, anything can be positively reinforcing in one set of conditions, and aversive in another. A pleasant pastime can become unpleasant when done to excess. A small piece of cake is good, but eating the whole cake can be disagreeable.

When you study, you sometimes engage in daydreaming. The change in your behavior is rewarding. But you can make daydreaming less attractive and at the same time reduce the amount of time you spend doing it. The next time that you are studying and you notice that your thoughts have drifted off the subject, get up from the desk and go to a quiet place with no distractions. Start daydreaming again and keep doing it awhile. It will not take long and you will soon notice that you are getting uncomfortable. Do not stop and go back to studying. Keep daydreaming until you get so bored with the activity that it becomes aversive. Doing this just once will not completely reduce the amount of time your mind wanders off a subject, but it will increase the negative aspects of daydreaming.

If you want to break a habit, do it to such an extent that you become sick of it. Smoking behavior is controllable through the process of satiation. An individual was allowed to smoke as many cigarettes as he wanted. Then the requirements were increased. He had to smoke as many cigarettes as possible until he got physically sick from them. He had to light a new one with the previous one. He was not to put them out, but to leave them burning in the ashtrays. At the end of the excess smoking period he got violently sick and was nauseated at just the smell of a cigarette. The next day the individual did not start smoking again.

To further reinforce the sickening aroma of the cigarettes, you can take a couple of butts from an ashtray and mix them with just a little water. Then you can put this mixture into a small container with a good lid. Every time you desire a smoke, open the lid and inhale the sickening fumes. This will reduce the desire for smoking.

The above example of the reduction of smoking through doing the behavior to excess is called "covert sensitization." It is a method that will allow you to break a habit quickly. The procedure involves the establishment of aversive mental associations.[3] Something that once was perceived as being pleasurable takes on disgusting attributes. Some extensions of this have included the reduction in eating by having the patients associate the sight of food with a lot of chicken droppings in a barnyard or some other equally revolting image.

Covert sensitization allows you to gain control of your behavior with your thoughts. Usually this is accomplished with satiation in the extreme. The desire for something should diminish in a direct relationship to your ability to imagine more and more disgusting things.

You might want to modify this procedure and use a technique that relies on positive and negative thought associations. Determine what the behavior is that you want to remove or modify. Develop some statements that are both positive and negative regarding that behavior. You can choose any number, but three positive and three negative is usually about the right number to be committed to memory. Repeat the statements to yourself twenty to thirty times a day, especially just before you actually engage in the behavior. Remember that you are not telling yourself that you will not engage in the behavior; just repeat the statements to yourself.

The following statements are ones that I have thought of concerning smoking behavior. Three statements are positive factors that I associate with smoking, and three of the statements are the negative factors that I associate with smoking. These are mine and do not necessarily have to be yours.

Smoking relaxes me.
Smoking leads to shortness of breath.
Smoking gives me something to do with my hands.
Smoking makes my breath smell horrible.
Smoking is an activity that some of my friends do.
Smoking costs me money.

Repeat these statements to yourself as you smoke. The reasoning behind this technique is that you are establishing a mental association between the positive and negative statements and your behavior. The internal processes are not clearly understood, but within a short time you will see a gradual falling off of smoking behavior. These statements will continually reinforce your future smoking behavior, and even the desire that you may have for a cigarette in the future will be reduced because of the statements and their associational values.

WITHDRAWAL OF REINFORCEMENT

Whenever you withdraw some reinforcer contingent upon some unwanted behavior, that response behavior is suppressed.

Barrett controlled a subject's nervous twitch by using a reinforcer chosen by the subject. Whenever the subject twitched, the music (reinforcement) was stopped. The withdrawal of the music was more effective than noise in reducing the unwanted response. The interruption of the music was made contingent upon the response which resulted in the tic's being reduced in frequency by almost 90 percent.[4] The reason that the patient's tics were reduced might be the result of his concentrated efforts at self-control.

Your self-control program could incorporate this technique

by establishing reinforcements and then making the receipt of them contingent upon the non-occurrence of the behavior. For example, if you smoked a cigarette today, then you could not watch any television tonight.

Behavior is not completely suppressed by removing a reinforcement contingent upon a behavior. If your motivational state for doing the behavior is high enough, it might be worthwhile to forgo a reinforcement in order to engage in that activity.

Confinement

To keep yourself from doing something you could lock yourself in a room. Confinement does not eliminate the behavior, but it can be used to prevent your doing it while you take other measures to control yourself. In the next chapter we will look at the ways that we can arrange the environment so that the chances for correctly controlling our behaviors are increased.

Obstacles in Your Path

Putting obstacles in the path of your desired behaviors is an effective technique for reducing the frequency of unwanted behaviors. The idea is not to deny yourself the ability to do the thing that you want to do, but to make it so much work that engaging in that activity is just not worth the trouble.

The obstacles in the path of the behavior should be instituted gradually instead of all at once. There should be a written schedule of when and how they shall be placed.

To reduce your smoking behavior you might want to place the following obstacles in front of each of the cigarettes that you want to smoke:

1. Write down the times and places of your desires for a smoke.
2. Write down the reasons for wanting this smoke.
3. Go to a place where there are no social reinforcers. (Do not smoke in the presence of others.)
4. Smoke only a brand that you do not especially like.
5. Repeat the positive and negative statements to yourself while you smoke.

Placing obstacles in front of the behavior reduces your desire for smoking. It is easier not to smoke than it is to go through all this.

The principle for reducing response frequencies with obstacles is not to deny the behavior completely, but instead to arrange the behaviors that will let you engage in the behavior.

A slightly different approach to the placing of obstacles in the path of a behavior is the technique of restricting where you can do the behavior. To cut down on your eating behavior, restrict eating to certain times of the day and only to certain specific places. Allow yourself a meal at night and at the table (without the television set being on).

INCOMPATIBLE RESPONSES

One of the most effective methods for reducing the frequency of an unwanted behavior is to condition a competing response. It is difficult to eat a chocolate pie while you are jogging in the park. You cannot smoke while you are sucking on a lollipop.

Each time you feel the desire to engage in the unwanted behavior, start doing something else. This allows you to modify the behavior immediately and completely. But the best thing about this method is that you can do something desirable and at the same time stop a habit. As long as you are able to immediately change to the competing response, the habit will not reappear.

CONCLUSIONS

Apparently once a standard of self-performance has been decided upon, activities that deviate from this plan will bring about negative feelings in you. A behavior can be controlled with negative self-feelings. You tend to stick to your self-improvement program because of your own self-will. Those actions that do not follow your self-prescribed plans can be met with aversive consequences. Punishments then may be used on ourselves to force behavioral compliance.

In this chapter several of the techniques that may be used

to reduce the occurrences of a behavior were discussed. The use of some of the negative procedures could be dangerous to both your emotional stability and to your physical body. Punishment seems especially difficult to justify for use with a self-control program. It may tend to exacerbate an already unsettled condition. The same conclusions may be reached with implosive therapy as a method for extinguishing an unwanted behavior.

The behavioral techniques that appear to offer safer and still effective methods for reducing an unwanted behavior are satiation, withdrawal of reinforcements, obstacles in the path of the behavior, and the conditioning of incompatible behaviors.

Your self-control should begin with the use of the positive methods of the previous chapter and the arrangement of the environment (discussed in the next chapter) before you set out to modify yourself with the negative procedures. If the effects of positive consequences are not effective in the control of your self, then use a combination of positive and negative procedures. The most permanent way to control your actions is through the use of reinforcing consequences that are positive. Anytime that you resort to an aversive consequence, be sure to allow yourself an alternative behavior with nonaversive consequences.

7

Environmental self-control

The environment controls you. But at the same time you can control various elements of the environment. You can so structure the world around you that you will receive rewards and reinforcements (and occasionally an aversive stimulation) for your behaviors. You can pick those behaviors that you want to reward or to punish, and you can make events in the environment contingent upon their occurring. It is the environment that allows you to develop self-control.

You are influenced by the results (consequences) of your actions. These consequences occur in the world that surrounds your behaviors. You can arrange for the taking of pills to alter your moods and behaviors. You can drink alcoholic beverages to cloud your mind from the pressures of the environment. You can alter your neurotic tendencies by visiting with psychiatrists and psychologists. You can improve your outlook on the world by taking a vacation. Some of the things that we do may temporarily alter our behaviors and reduce our sensibilities (taking tranquilizers), but they are likely to lead to long-term psychological deterioration. A vacation may bring about only a partial improvement in ourselves, or one lasting only until we get back into town.

If we can arrange the environmental factors that shape our behaviors so that we are positively controlled, it will be possible to bring about lasting self-improvement. We can influence ourselves to emit the proper behaviors if we are successful in establishing the proper environment in which those desired behaviors may occur.

If the environment controls your behavior, how can you have any real self-control? Will you become just a machine that responds to the pressures of the world? Although behavioral tendencies are influenced by the environmental contingencies, you can arrange the events so that you are able to get what you want. If you want to control your sleeping behavior, you set an alarm clock. Just as you are able to arrange the environmental event to control your behavior with a clock, you can do the same with other factors in the environment for other behaviors. The world does not completely control your actions. You can turn off the alarm in the morning and go back to sleep. Or you may decide the night before not to bother with the alarm and get up whenever you feel like it.

Self-control procedures will allow you to disconnect the environmental contingencies from yourself. You decide upon the limits of behavioral dependence and you can remove yourself from their influences at any time that you desire.

You should try to structure your self-control environment to help you to modify behaviors. The environment controls your behavior because of the following:

1. There are consequences for the behaviors that you engage in.
2. These effects of your behaviors arise from the environment in which the behaviors have been emitted.
3. The environment contingencies do not occur until some behavior has been accomplished.

A Total Immersion

B. F. Skinner suggested in *Walden Two* that artists and other creative people be free of the necessity of making a living while they pursue their careers. To help you in attaining your goal it is better to have a completely structured environment in which all factors and contingencies are channeling your behavior toward that end. For a writer this would mean that all his behaviors should be channeled toward putting words on paper. Everything that the writer does should be aimed at finishing the book or article. The person should not have to have his attentions divided among diverse activities like work, paying the rent, or washing the dishes. The environment around the writer should be void of all nonwriting stimuli. The room should not have televisions, radios, nonessential books, telephones, or friends.

The total commitment to a behavioral goal should include an environment so structured so as to reinforce behaviors toward that end. If a person is sincere about cutting down on eating, he does not establish an environment in which food is all around him. To totally commit oneself to a diet means that the world of food is restricted. To decide that you will reach a certain goal means that you must arrange your environment to minimize the chance that you will engage in nongoal activities.

When Dr. Joyce Brothers decided to enter the television game show "The $64,000 Question," she picked a topic that she knew little about. She felt that she had a better chance to become a contestant if her chosen subject was the sport of boxing. Her goal was to learn everything that there was to know about boxing. She arranged her environment so that all her behaviors were shaped to the acquisition of boxing facts. Every waking hour was spent in learning about boxing. At breakfast her husband would fire questions at her about the sport: "Who was the referee in this fight?" "How many rounds did this fight go?' "'How much does a middleweight boxer weigh?" She saw all the fight films that she could get. Nothing but boxing occupied her attention for several months. According to the goal that she had set for herself, these efforts paid off. She won the contest.

Many people do the same thing to reach their goals. They go into seclusion and put all their attentions into a particular activity. For some it is a function of the way they normally work, and for others it is because of the pressure that the environment places on them. But most people are not so lucky to have months of time that can be used to engage in one activity. We still need to work in order to pay for the food we eat. We need periods of social activities. Sometimes we have to schedule periods for exercises. As you develop your personal program for self-control, you need to consider the problem of arranging the environment so that some behaviors are controlled while at the same time you need to consider the impact on the other things that you do.

An Aversive Environment

A real problem for self-control is an aversive world. In a study of the effects of environmental noise on intellectual behavior it has been shown that the louder the nose the harder it is to control one's improvement. Children on the ground floor of a high rise apartment building did worse in school than did children higher up in the same building. The children on the first few floors were constantly exposed to the noise of a congested street, while the ones higher up were relatively free from the street noises.

Sharp, sudden, and loud noises cause physiological reactions in our bodies. A sudden noise causes a fear reaction. Adrenaline is released into the bloodstream when an organism is exposed to noises. A constant exposure to irritating noises has been shown to cause stress symptoms and eventually high blood pressure. We can learn to adjust to a steady noise. We adapt to background noises as long as they are relatively constant. If your environment is filled with loud and sudden noises, there is a technique that you can use that will mask the aversive environmental noise. This technique operates on the physiological principle of adaptation in hearing. A fan will generate what is called "white noise." The steady hum of an air conditioner fan drowns out the external noises. A white noise generator may make it possible for you to create an environment more conducive to studying by eliminating distractions.

If an urban environment of smog, traffic noises, crime, crowded conditions, and city taxes diverts your attention from self-improvement, you can always move out of the environment and live in the country. On the other hand, if a rural environment makes you feel unchallenged and unstimulated by a seeming lack of intellectual challenges, you can always move to the city. Changing our geographical location is one way of restructuring the environment that affects the way in which we behave.

The same principle of changing the environment holds true when we look at our vocational environment. If the job is getting to you and causing you to feel that you are wasting your life, then a consideration of a new career is in order. Feeling that you never get any recognition for your efforts is a sign that another occupation or place of work may be called for. Changing jobs will do a lot for the way you behave. Many individuals have been forced to change jobs. These people have come alive when they got into their new jobs. They may have spent years doing something they hated, only to find that their entire outlook on the world changed drastically when they got into a career suited to them. It has been an accepted fact that doing something that you do not like can affect your health. Many people find themselves wanting to be sick rather than having to go to work while others are so happy with their jobs that they never miss a day of work due to sickness.

To change your career requires a little planning and some self-control. Education seems to be the best way of altering one's career. It takes self-control to go to night school or to take a correspondence course. But the benefits that can be derived from additional education may be worth the effort involved.

People are products of the environment in which they live. The social environment is a powerful influence upon behavior. The power of a peer group in shaping a young person's behavior is well known. The chances that a child will become a criminal are greatly increased when he lives in a ghetto. The possibilities for associating with the wrong kind of friends in the ghetto are higher than in other areas. A child who grows up in a low crime area and who has friends that are not criminal in nature has a better chance of being a worthwhile citizen than a ghetto child.

We can control the social environment in which we live. We

can choose our friends. We can select people to associate with who have the necessary characteristics that will channel our behaviors to the proper goals.

We are only as good as the friends and colleagues with whom we associate. Prisons are effective in controlling behavior just as long as the individuals are kept within the walls. Whenever the inmates are released to go back to their previous environments, the controls on behaviors are discontinued. The social pressures of the gang then take over the shaping of individuals' behaviors. This is one of the reasons for the high rates of recidivism in the United States. The criminal environment is not changed. People are allowed to go back to the same environment that shaped their previous criminal activities. It is not the learning that committing a crime may lead to a prison sentence that has the greatest effect on behavior, but it is the social environment that shapes the behaviors more effectively.

Use as much care as you can to pick the social environment with which you interact. The results will make or break a self-control program.

The Self-Improvement Box

The Skinner Box is an experimental device that controls environmental influences and shapes behaviors. These boxes have been used by psychologists to control, shape, and modify the responses of various subjects. The Skinner Box makes it possible to control any extraneous stimuli that might affect an experiment. The device also can be used to teach various behaviors through the use of reinforcements (both positive and negative). The animal is placed in the cage that is bare except for some mechanism that can be operated by the animal and a hole where food can be delivered.

The experimenter can select the schedule of when the animal will be reinforced. The animal makes some responses, usually involving the use of the mechanism in the cage, and is reinforced. The reinforcements are used to condition the animal in acquiring the proper responses. A motivated rat (one that has been deprived of food for awhile) can be taught certain behaviors if he is placed in a Skinner Box. The controlled environment restricts the number of competing responses that the animal can make, and the deliverance of the reinforcements allows for rapid and constant learning of the required behavior.

There is a larger form of the Skinner Box located in Nevada. These boxes have few doors, no windows, no clocks, and few distractions. These are places that have been built by casino owners so as to reduce the number of alternative responses that can be made while in the casino. The gambling environment is well controlled. The reinforcements seem to occur just often enough to keep people in the casinos for long periods of time without extinguishing their gambling behaviors. Just as psychologists have been able to develop controlled environments to manipulate the behaviors of their subjects, casino owners have been able to arrange an environment conducive to the maintenance of gambling behaviors.

You can do the same thing to control your own behaviors as have the psychologists and casino owners. You can arrange the environment so that it becomes a self-control box for your self-improvement. The idea is to develop stimulus control. You must structure the environment so that your behavior falls under its control. You regulate your behavior by altering the stimulus environment. When you want to stop watching the television, you can sell the set.

Behavior-modification principles tell us that if we want to engage in some activity we must fix the environment so that we will be most likely to do it. If one needs to practice a musical instrument, but finds many excuses for not doing it, then altering the environment will help in controlling that activity. Take a chair, the musical instrument, a timer, and go to an empty corner of the house. Go where there are no distractions. The idea is to find the environment where nothing else will interfere with the practice. It would be best to be able to go to a completely empty room and lock yourself in, but an empty corner is almost as good.

Hanging up a sheet around you is another way to reduce distracting stimuli. It is the objects in the environment that are cues for certain of your behaviors. This means that a magazine is meant to be read, and a television that is on is meant to be watched. Whenever you find yourself being distracted by the objects in the environment around you, remove them or hide them. You are less likely to think about food when you are not constantly exposed to the sight of pies, cakes, candy, or even the refrigerator.

Arranging Your Environment

There are several techniques for arranging the environment so that our behaviors will be properly influenced by it. One way is to move to a new neighborhood, change jobs, find new friends, move into a new home. Another technique involves restructuring the present elements of the environment. You can restrict behaviors to certain times and places. Do not watch television before eleven-thirty at night.

Restructuring the place in which you live can control your behaviors. Interior decorators claim that a person's moods are affected by the arrangement, color, and style of the room furnishings. A yellow wall creates a different image than does a black one. A somber, colorless room may create depression.

If an environment is to control your behavior, it must be used. Also, it is more effective to structure an environment for one activity and use it only for that purpose. Remember if you work in one place, find another spot in which to play. If you intend that a desk should be used to work on, then do not engage in other activities at the desk. The association must be between the desk and expected work.

You can create for yourself an environment for work. Purchase a desk. Place it in an isolated part of the house or apartment. Remove all distractions that may come into the line of sight. Take down all pictures and remove any nearby radio or television sets. Put nothing on the desk that is not directly related to the work that you intend to do there. Decide upon the times when you will work at the desk. Follow your personal self-control contract and you have created an environment that will maintain the desired behavior. If at any time while you are in this environment, you are distracted, get up and go to another area. If you suddenly find yourself daydreaming when you are supposed to be reading, studying, or writing, then go somewhere else and daydream for awhile.

If you do not have the room to set up a separate place for your work behaviors, you can establish a stimulus control situation in another way. Buy a brightly colored rug or sheet that you can place over the top of the kitchen table or the desk in the den. When the time for work arrives, spread the colored cover over the desk or table and begin to work for the required amount of time. When you have finished the task, remove the cover and put it away until the next day. The purpose of this is to create an association between the stimulus object and the desired behavior. Do not use the colored cover for anything but the one task you have chosen it for. You might want to use other colored sheets or covers for different jobs. Also, you might want to expand this idea to the area around the desk. Hanging the colored sheets around the desk as well as putting one on the desk's surface will help to establish stimulus control for your behaviors.

How to Be Forced to Work

The proper use of the environment will force you to work. Environmental controls will help you to organize and manage your time more efficiently.

In order to write a book a writer must spend many hours putting words on paper. An artist must spend time getting the desired forms and colors onto a canvas. A businessman has to spend long hours in becoming successful. But each may procrastinate. He may structure his environment so that there are numerous reasons for not doing something right away. We can arrange the environment so that nonessential activities will not be engaged in. The signals that are put out by the environment influence your thoughts and your behaviors. Sitting in a room with a television set causes you to think about watching it. Or the sight of a picture of relatives that you have not called in a long time may make you drop what you are doing and go to see them. Environmental objects control your actions in ways that may not be the best for self-improvement.

A friend of mine decided that the only way that he was going to get any work done was to remove all the tempting stimuli. He could not work at home. The ringing phone, the kids, the distractions did not let him engage in the activities that he wanted to. As soon as he sat down there would be another request for his time. He rented an inexpensive apartment where he could go and work. It had a desk, a chair, an electric light, a few writing supplies, and little else. He hung a rug over the only window and told no one where the apartment was. When he goes there he has nothing to do but work. He has successfully arranged his environment to control his work behavior. He goes there every day and stays four hours. He does all his work in this apartment. He does no researching, television watching, eating, socializing, sleeping, or card playing there.

It is my friend's willpower that makes him go to this apartment day after day. It is his power of self-control that puts him into the room those four hours. Otherwise, he is completely free to leave at any time.

A structured environment such as that described above can be effective in controlling the behaviors of studying, creative thinking, inventing, reading, memory practice, painting, writing—the list is endless. The principle to follow in developing such an environment for yourself is to establish conditions where only the desired activity can be engaged in.

Imitation

Structuring the proper environment should include people as well as objects. We can follow the examples of others and modify our behaviors. All that is necessary is to find a model that has those characteristics that you deem worthy of your emulation and pattern your behavior after it.

Learning is increased through the process of imitating the behavior of others. In fact, learning a language would be impossible if it were not for the ability to mimic the speech of another person. Motor skills are acquired through the use of models. Also, watching the behavior of someone else allows us to adapt to new situations.

Your ability to control your own behaviors will be influenced and enhanced by the observation of people who you consider to have exemplary behaviors. Experimental studies have shown that we adopt the behavioral standards of others and we evaluate our self-controls relative to that standard.[1] If you choose a poorly performing model, your behavior is going to be poor because of the mediocre standard you have established for your self-control.

Select a hardworking, consistent person to match your behavior with. Establish standards based upon that person's performances. You can then judge your behavior in terms of those with whom you have chosen to associate or even a model whom you have never met. The people whom you use to model your behaviors after may be just those you have seen in the movies, on television, or have read about in the newspapers. You do not have to interact with them to be able to copy their behaviors.

The imitation of others can also help you to reduce the occurrence of behaviors. Seeing someone else given aversive consequences (being punished) is effective in keeping you from doing that behavior.

Tools for Self-Control

The objects that are in your environment control your behaviors. You can choose the objects that will control you in the way that you want to be shaped. People use things to control themselves. If you want to get up in the mornings, you set an alarm. We use fans to keep us cool. Telephones allow us to talk to people. The objects of the environment should be used as tools that allow us to extend our capabilities. Tools are selected to make life better.

The following are some of the tools that may make it easier for you to control your behaviors. This is by no means a complete list because there are many things that you may feel are suited to your self-improvement program that I have not included.

Reinforcements—anything in the environment may be selected as a reward for your behaviors. Anything that you like may be a positive reinforcement. It must follow response.

Aversive stimuli—anything in the environment that you dislike may reduce the frequency of behaviors.

Food and drink—are effective in establishing motivation for you to do something.

Electric fans—may be used to drown out extraneous noises and create a stimulus situation more conducive to some forms of behavior, i.e., studying and reading.

Curtains, sheets, and other various colored materials—may be used to establish various stimulus control situations for different self-control activities.

Tape recorders—play messages, to help you to relax with a prerecorded message, and a great many other self-control purposes.

Alarm clocks—signal the end of an interval time period.

Wrist counters—help you keep exact count of the number of times you have emitted a particular behavior during the day.

Electric timers—may be used for many things such as turning off and on reinforcers, i.e., the television.

Plastic counters—the small ones that you can stick into your shirt pocket will allow you to keep track of your daily responses.

Blood pressure gauge—to allow you to monitor the effects of self-relaxation.

Reading pacer—as I was glancing through a copy of *Popular Science* I saw an advertisement for a device to control one's reading speed. It is adjustable from 250 to 650 words per minute. It was advertised for $1.00 each. Check the advertisements for firms that offer surplus merchandise. There may be a tool that will be just the thing to give you complete control over your behaviors.

Headphones—allow you to listen to music as background noise and at the same time reduce extraneous noises.

Bell timers—these mechanical devices can be used to time your behaviors independently of electrical sources.

Stopwatches—may be used to time your reading speeds and any number of other activities.

Graph paper—chart your self-improvement progress.

8

Control your health

Your health can sometimes be what you think it is. There are many illnesses that have been brought about by an individual's mind. Psychosomatic illnesses are thought-controlled. Diseases such as allergies, asthma, diarrhea, migraines, obesity, peptic ulcers, and tics are often controlled by mental processes. You can affect your health by the things that you do. A lifetime of drinking can cause cirrhosis of the liver (among other things). The harmful effects of smoking are numerous. Many other of your behaviors can lead to diseases of the body.

Your mind can also affect the body's health indirectly through more subtle activities than overt behaviors. Hypochondria is an emotional illness that shows itself in a wide range of disturbances. Hypochondriacs do not fake their pains. Their reports about the way the feel are not make-believe but real. Hypochondriasis is a reaction to stressful situations. Events in their environments cause individuals emotional stress that is reflected in their imagined illnesses. The loss of a job, death in the family, or legal problems are emotional factors that cause illnesses in some people. Frequently, mental depression shows itself in symptoms that lack a physical cause. Your emotional responses to the environment may lead to physiological sicknesses.

The mind creates illnesses even when there is no underlying physical problems. The effects of the mind are sometimes stronger than medicines. The whole area of psychosomatic health may be summarized by the following statement: "I think I am going to be sick today—and to think about it, I really do not feel very good right now."

☀ Self-control means that you have the power within you to control, modify, and shape your behaviors. A self-improvement program should also consider the aspects of health as well as behaviors. The self-control of health involves the arrangement of contingencies so that illnesses may be brought under stimulus control. The purpose of this chapter is to get you to think about the relationship of your emotional and mental states to your health. Health is just another behavior that can be controlled through the proper applications of behavior-modification principles.

This chapter is highly controversial. I suggest that before you attempt to correct a disease that you have with the techniques presented here, you check with a physician to make sure that you are not going to aggravate an unstable condition.

The mind influences the health of the body. We think ourselves into many illnesses. Many times there are no disease germs to blame for the deterioration of parts of the body. What germ got into the intestines and ate a small hole through the wall? We call this condition a peptic ulcer. It is caused by emotional reactions to the environment, not by germs.

Serious bodily reactions have been the indirect result of people's reactions to environmental pressures. The stressful situations of the office, the job, the relationships with others, and, in general, the pressure-cooker of modern living cause excessive changes in the physiological balance of the body. This unbalance is mind-controlled. Perceptions of environmental stress cause the endocrine system to set up bodily defense mechanisms. Put people into pressure situations, and stress them to the ends of their endurances for several years, and you will succeed in getting individuals with acid in their stomachs, holes in the walls of their intestines, heartburns, and sour dispositions.

The power of suggestion can affect the health of people.

Having two or three people tell you that you do not look at all well and maybe you should have stayed home in bed is enough to make your throat a little sore. It only takes a few remarks from others to convince many people they do not feel as well as when they got up. Casual remarks affect one's health. All that is necessary is to get a person's mind thinking about an illness and in a short time he starts to become ill.

The theme of this chapter is that the mind can control the health of a person. If we can think ourselves into a condition, then it is possible to use the techniques and principles of behavior modification to bring about good health.

PLACEBOS

Doctors sometimes give patients fake pills so that the patients will feel better. There is nothing in a placebo to make a person any better. The patients are told that the pills will cure their illness if they take them for a few days. If they do not feel better at the end of the period, the doctor tells them to come back for a further examination or more fake pills. The patients are not told that they are taking fake pills. Even though the pills have nothing in them to cure any illness, the patients many times report that they feel much better (thanks to the pills the doctor prescribed). It is not the placebo that cures the illness. The cure is in the patients' minds.

A placebo, or fake pill, allows the mind to control the body. In hundreds of studies with the use of placebos, pain due to illness has been significantly reduced. Investigations of sclerosis, migraines, colds, constipation, and asthma show that placebos reduce the symptoms and even "cure" the disease. Since the above diseases are often brought about by the person's mind, it seems logical that they can be removed by the person's mind.

Patients who have taken placebos even report the negative side effects that normally accompany a "real" drug. It appears that the emotional states and mental beliefs of an individual can make an inert drug potent.

Despite the large amount of experimental and clinical evidence on placebo effectiveness in controlling pain and curing illnesses, the placebo has been ignored by both physicians and pharmaceutical firms. Real drugs have chemical effects. What gives the placebo its effect?[1] Your mind.

Disease Mentality

There is a theory that disease germs are constantly present. The reason that we come down with diseases at different times is supposedly due to physiological changes in the body's immunity system. The defense agents that guard against the incorporation or attack of disease germs are controlled by the brain. Minor changes in the environment and the subtle influences on the physiological balance of the body influence the susceptibility to diseases.

Friedman, Ader, and Glasgow stressed mice for three days, inoculated them with a virus, and stressed them for another four days.[2] Another group of rats was stressed for the same amount of time but did not receive the shot of virus. A third group was given just the inoculation of the virus but with no stress. The group that was merely stressed did not get the disease. The group that was just inoculated (no stress) did not get the disease. Only the group that was stressed *and* received the virus got the disease.

If we are able to show that illness requires not only an infectious agent but also mental influences, it becomes apparent that our response to stress is important in our susceptibility to diseases. The common cold may be nothing more than a mental attitude that we will now allow ourselves to get sick. Many individuals have been examined by their doctors and found to be in great health. But later stressful changes in the individuals' lives have caused severe physical and physiological reactions to occur.[3] Reactions to the environment affect hormonal balances that in turn affect physiological processes.

Asthma

Asthma attacks are controlled through processes of the mind. Asthma is a disease that is not transmitted from one individual to another. It affects the lungs and can cause permanent damage.

The asthmatic has difficulty getting air into and out of the lungs. It appears that for some reason the smooth muscles of the lungs close down down the passageways of the bronchioli resulting in stale air being trapped in the lungs. Breathing becomes difficult. There is a feeling of suffocation that leads to more stress and tension in the individual.

Some of the outside agents known to bring on asthma attacks are: pine trees, dust, feathers, molds, pollen, carpets, and cats. Before you start thinking that there may be something in these substances that causes a physiological reaction in the body, let us look at some that are not likely to emit physical allergens. There are documented cases of asthma being induced in patients by the following things: radio speeches, bicycle races, police vans, and even pictures of pine trees. Asthma is a disorder that is responsive to a substance, an object, an extrinsic event, or a mental symbol.

Asthma seems to come and go without outside influences. It is responsive to suggestion but only temporarily. Intense stressful situations do not always bring on asthmatic attacks. But whenever stress is used in conjunction with a known precipitant, asthma attacks occur.

Air pollution causes asthma in some people. Dust causes asthma. Dust is the result of volcanic activity, forest fires, industry, vehicle exhausts, and pollen. About seventy tons of dust fall on a square mile of New York City each month; in Los Angeles the estimate is thirty-five tons. Some heavy industrial areas have 200 tons of dust per square mile every month.

The amount of particles in the air is a good indicator of pollution. Cities have an average of 150,000 nuclei particles per cubic centimeter; countrysides have 10,000; and mountaintops have 4,000. The outdoors has usually half the amounts found in homes and offices.

Bacteria counts vary directly with the number of particles found in the air. If asthmatic reactions are brought about by the combination of stress and pollution found in the city, the best way to control it is to move to the top of a mountain. Moving sometimes may be the best answer since asthma has no cure and drugs such as theophylline only relieve one of the discomforts associated with the symptoms.

STRESS

Even though stressful situations do not directly precipitate asthmatic attacks, there is a cause-effect relationship between it and other physiological problems. Disruptive factors in daily life cause stress. With continual stress the chances increase that a person will contract a stress-type illness.

The environment is responsible for causing stress. Bodily reactions have been known to occur from getting a divorce, being fired, having a death in the family, or being presented with situations that are too difficult to cope with. The more the change in one's life, the more emotion-ridden the situations are, the higher the chance that illnesses will result.

Situations involving anxiety, fear, or even loud noises can bring on physiological reactions. These bodily responses are automatically established to "fight" or to "flee" the threat. The cerebral cortex becomes excited and sends a message to the adrenal glands to produce an adrenal hormone. This hormone is a stress agent that changes the body's processes—respiration, heart rate, blood pressure, blood flows. The stage is set for running away or putting up a fight. Crowded, tense, and hurried living produces situations that stress the body processes. We cannot stay at a state of heightened readiness for long periods of time without some harmful effects. Prolonged periods of stress from environment lead to cardiovascular illness, asthma, ulcers, and other diseases.

The relationship between emotional stress and bodily disease has been an accepted fact for a long time. The hard-paced business world, with its considerable tension-causing activities, takes its toll of many individuals by giving them ulcers. The gastrointestinal tract is the most susceptible to emotional stress. Daily stresses result in heartburns, and ulcers are the result of the increased flow of stomach acid.

How does one keep from getting ulcers? Live far away from civilization. Enter into no activities involving hostility, aggression, or excessive competition with others. Since most of us still want to live in a stressful environment (it may be more fun than living alone on a mountain), we need to arrange the contingencies of the environment to reduce the effects of stress on our bodies. Maybe it will not be possible to remove the stress-causing situations, but we can do certain things to reduce the damage that stress does to our bodies.

Diets are effective in reducing our physiological reactions to stress. The Japanese people react little to stress. Their environment is crowded, tense, stressful, and they live fast-paced, hectic lives. Yet their stress incidence is quite low. The Finnish people have a high level of heart disease. This is due in large part to their diets since they lead lives that are free of stress. (It also may be a hereditary factor.)

How does one reduce the effects of stress on the body? By learning to relax and by learning to play hard. Preliminary conclusions from recent research show that an involvement in competitive sports reduces physiological reactions to stressful situations. Periods of overtaxation of the body followed by periods of complete relaxation will reduce the effects of stress. Work hard but play hard. Learning to relax, taking time to plan ahead, avoiding fatty foods, stopping smoking, and playing hard will reduce your tensions.

HIGH BLOOD PRESSURE

An indirect result of the pressures of daily living is high blood pressure. High blood pressure is controlled by the brain. It is easily controlled and diagnosed. But if it is not spotted and treated it can ruin your heart, eyes, kidneys, and even your life. Twenty-eight million people in the United States have this disease. Many of the people have excessive blood pressure because of the way they perceive the world and how they attempt to counteract the stressful situations they find themselves in.

A permanent cure for hypertension is not known, but the controls for it are available. Drugs and present treatments for the disease are only delaying strategies, but the lower the blood pressure the better the chance for a longer life.

Cardiovascular diseases affected nearly 30 million people in the United States in 1973. This illness accounts for more than half of all deaths. Stress is the most likely cause of this problem. Some physicians may suggest self-control programs to be used in conjunction with prescribed medicines, but even without self-controls, modern medicine can treat every case of high blood pressure.

High blood pressure can cause tension headaches and migraines. Although the primary cause of these headaches has not been proven, they are usually associated with excessive blood flow in the region of the scalp. Migraines are the result of attempts to counteract the effects of the blood pressure by constantly contracting the muscles in the neck and forehead. Relaxation techniques of self-control are likely to aid in the lowering of the blood pressure. Also, self-control procedures will bring about muscle relaxation. Both these results will lessen the severity of tension headaches.

There are many individuals that portray an exterior coolness in face of pressure, but they have high blood pressure just like the person who shows his worries. Persons that are laid off suffer an increase in their blood pressures that persists until they are able to start working again. Employment is but one cure for this problem. Diets low in salt are commonly prescribed. Surgery has been performed on individuals to cut specific nerves leading to the chest. Some people have moved from the pressure-ridden cities. But mostly people try to hang onto their hectic lives and hope for the best. People may come to expect high levels of stressful conditions and are reluctant to move.

Relaxation methods are especially effective in reducing high blood pressure. Relaxation therapy can be self-controlled and self-monitored. The problem that occurs often is that the patients quit practicing their self-control techniques. People have been told that unless they follow a program of relaxation and medicine, their blood pressure will rise dangerously high. To stay with a program for controlling blood pressure requires self-control, which takes willpower.

A recent method for controlling blood pressure is biofeedback. This method will be described more fully in the next chapter. Biofeedback teaches one bodily control. The use of biofeedback machines has successfully reduced the blood pressures of patients who have been troubled with that problem for years.[4]

Biofeedback is not the complete answer to high blood pressure. The method is temporary. As soon as the patient is disconnected from the biofeedback machine, he is unable to determine his performance levels and the pressure rises again. We depend upon some form of feedback to let us know where the blood pressure stands, and without that feedback we have no control.

Recently another technique has been added to the list of methods for controlling heartbeats and blood pressure. It has been known that when seals dive under the water, their hearts slow down and blood is increasingly channeled to the brain. This is known as the "diving reflex" and recent experiments have shown that the same effects occur whenever human beings dunk their heads into pans of ice water. Within half a minute of being dunked, the person's heartbeats are significantly reduced. Under the supervision of physicians, patients have been taught this technique as a self-control method that can be used at home without drugs.

To practice diving to reduce your blood pressure may be dangerous. A physician is needed to determine the health and stamina of the heart. Stress is brought to bear on the heart by diving and this could bring about a heart attack. This new technique is one that you can use with self-treatment for problems diagnosed and supervised by a doctor.

Self-Control Methods for Good Health

Many chronic illnesses, such as asthma, cirrhosis, high blood pressure, and headaches, will yield to various medical controls (drugs, hospitalization—removes the patient from a stressful situation—and psychological counseling), but the symptoms quickly return whenever the patient reenters the environment that caused his disorders in the first place.

Overactivity leads to physiological imbalances that lead to somatic problems like: chronic tension, anxiety reactions, digestive problems, breathing difficulties, and irregularities. Drugs are effective temporarily. If these psychosomatic illnesses could be brought under some kind of stimulus control, then self-control methods could be established for long-lasting treatment without drugs. Our reactions to environmental factors must be controlled. And this means self-control. The American Heart Association has written: "Only the individual can alter his own emotional reaction to daily events."

A healthy attitude has much to do with one's abilities to resist diseases and to feel good in stressful situations. Although not an overt behavior, a vibrant outlook on life is generally recognized to be an important element in the control of health. A healthy view of life can be developed by establishing environmental contingencies.

Rosenberg has conducted experiments that have shown that positive statements that subjects have thought up on their own affect their attitudes and beliefs.[5] Developing a list of reasons for feeling good will cause you to feel better. Self-persuasive arguments for healthy self-attitudes may be similar to the following. This list is a short compilation of my reasons for feeling good.

    1. By feeling good I will spend less money on physicians.

    2. I will spend less money and have less dependence upon drugs.

    3. I will have more time to do the things that I really like to do.

    4. I will have less physiological reactions to stress.

    5. By being able to control my health successfully, I will feel more confident with my ability to modify other aspects of my behavior.

Another technique for developing a cheerful and healthy attitude is to work at a job that you like, that you are suited for, and from which you are able to get the proper recognition. Breer and Locke have found through their research that individuals are able to modify their own attitudes through a rewarding job or task.⁶ This improvement in attitude generalized to other areas of the individuals' lives. Arranging one's work environment is a good way to modify an attitude toward life. A person who is continually gratified with his career—it is an extension of his lifestyle, and others recognize his value—will have his healthy attitude reinforced daily. The behaviors that he emits are favorably received. Whenever a person hates his job, his mental health is bound to suffer. Why suffer when it is much easier to arrange the contingencies of the world to reward you for the things that you like to do? Life is too short and time is too priceless to waste in an activity that is not rewarding. To develop self-control for your feelings and for your health, search for new adventures for the body and the mind. Put some value and meaning into your life by finding something worthwhile to do.

The evidence from the work of Breer and Locke indicates what we have thought for a long time—our inner beliefs and feelings are directly influenced by the feedback that we get from the world around us. Thus, permanent and positive self-evaluations can be established with the arrangement of positive environmental contingencies—get a good job that is an extension of yourself.

The following list contains the principles of behavior modification that can be applied to modify one's health. Before you do anything else, get the advice of a doctor. Do not risk making an erroneous diagnosis and causing greater harm by trying to be your own physician.

1. Decide on what aspect of your health you are going to concentrate your efforts. Be specific. Set up a control program to reduce your weight by twenty pounds, instead of a general program of "I will feel lighter."

2. What behaviors must be emitted in order to modify and control that specific part of my health? You should consider whether these behaviors are controllable by you and if they are repeatable activities. Behaviors that could be considered under this category may be similar to the following:

Methods of relaxation.
Controlling smoking or drinking.

Exercises.
Sports.
Proper dieting.

3. You should establish an explicit goal that you will strive toward. The previous behaviors should lead one to the achievement of the selected goal.

4. Write out the schedule for the attainment and sign it as you would a contract.

5. Be consistent; do not let a day slip by without sticking to your plan.

6. Arrange the environmental contingencies so that you will be more likely to emit the proper behaviors.

7. The development of self-controls for health must be kept to small units of change; and these behavioral changes must be kept gradual.

8. Keep objective records on a daily basis.

9. Use self-monitoring tools so that you can determine precisely your self-improvements.

10. Develop the ability to completely relax and reduce the harmful effects of stress situations. (See the chapter on relaxation and self-hypnosis in this book.)

11. Develop a vibrant and healthy attitude toward life. List the arguments for feeling good. Find the career that best suits you.

12. Develop self-confidence by learning the techniques for self-control that are presented in this book.

Danger

The treatment of diseases requires physicians. It is foolish and dangerous to diagnose yourself. Modifying the beat of your heart may overtax it. Controlling brainwaves may cause an epileptic attack. Of course, there is always that chance that you will try to cure the wrong problem.

A researcher successfully taught rats to control their heart beats. Twenty percent of the rats that learned to control their heart rates later died of heart failure! Of the other 80 percent, a large number developed serious cardiac problems. None of the rats in a control group were taught to control their heart rates, and none of these animals developed or died from heart troubles.

The clinical data is fairly conclusive—many diseases have been controlled through the application of behavior-modification techniques. But the possibility for self-harm from the incorrect use of these procedures is important to consider.

9

Biological monitoring and feedback

Individuals have been taught with operant-conditioning techniques and electronic devices to control various body organs and functions. Behavior-modification procedures enhanced with devices developed by electronic engineers have successfully controlled chronic tension, anxiety, gastrointestinal disorders, heartbeats and rates, blood pressure, and even the electrical rhythms of the human brain.

Control of the body's autonomic functions is made possible only when the individual is aware of bodily activities. In this chapter, the use of these devices to monitor the inner workings of your body will be explored. Without the aid of biofeedback machines, learning to change the beat of a heart would be as difficult as learning to play basketball while blindfolded. It might be done, but only with years of concentrated practice. It takes the Yogi of India years of dedicated practice to arrive at their level of self-control.

Your self-control of your body and your mind will have far-ranging and long-lasting effects on your life. With the proper feedback techniques, you can develop relaxation, reduce the effects of stress, lower blood pressure, be more creative, and stand a much better chance of living longer and better.

Biofeedback

Biofeedback machines pick up and amplify the minute signals generated by the cells in the brain or the muscles of the body. Biofeedback training operates on the principle that if we can be made aware of the existence of these small electrical discharges, we can learn to control their occurrences. To learn any skill we must know how we are doing. In learning to control your overt behaviors, you counted them when they occurred and plotted them on graphs. The record of the behaviors on the charts served as a warning if your actions were getting worse; or, if there was any improvement, the charts would serve as a form of self-reinforcement.

To learn to control one's body and brainwaves, a person needs something that will give him knowledge of his performance—a biofeedback machine does this. With the right equipment you can gain a mastery of your biological system. You can control just about anything that emits any kind of signal. This biological control can be achieved in less than a couple of hours.

There are several companies that are building biofeedback machines. These machines have been developed for use in medical offices and at home. They range in price from $19.95 (quality uncertain) to units costing $10,000. The cheaper the unit the less likely that it will be able to discern the proper signals for you to develop self-control. Some of these devices have been called "alpha machines" because of the manufacturers' claims that their machines are able to monitor the alpha rhythm of the brain.

Biofeedback devices are just tools that can be used for self-control. With operant-conditioning techniques we can develop control over internal states as well as over our behaviors. These operant procedures when used with biofeedback machines are just as effective as drugs in the treatment of several diseases. Biofeedback control has the added benefit of being nonaddictive.

Biological Control

Biofeedback devices will allow you to develop control over your heart, digestion, and kidneys in the same manner that you can learn to control any other form of your behavior—through feedback.

The mystics of the Orient have had this kind of internal control for a long time. They learned their control through years of concentrated practice, that involved controlled breathing, relaxation, and the directed concentration on specific objects in the environment. The teachings of Zen use the principle of feedback to teach self-control.

The electronic surveillance of the body allows a monitoring of the involuntary system. Blood pressure, skin temperature, heartbeats, and individual nerve and motor units[1] have been conditioned with biofeedback devices. For anyone who wants to learn, the equipment is available that will allow the monitoring of almost any internal biological condition. The present level of electronic technology can be used to detect the smallest of internal activities, which means that given the equipment we can control about any biological activity that we want to.

Since biofeedback can be used with good success to control the level of relaxation in muscles, the technique is well adapted to reducing stress tensions. Asthma, tension headaches, high blood pressure, and many other things have been treated successfully with biofeedback machines.

Heart Rates and Blood Pressure

Subjects have been taught to use biofeedback to control their heart rates and blood pressures, and to smooth out irregularities of the heart. Blood pressure and heart rates have been controlled independently of each other.

Heart patients with severe arrhythmic patterns have used biofeedback so well in controlling their problems that they have stopped using drugs. Some studies have shown that with biofeedback training, subjects can bring about a 25-percent change (faster or slower) in their heart rates. Increases or decreases in the number of beats have approached twenty per minute.

Patients are wired up to electroencephalographs that have been specially fitted with a device to signal the heart rate. The signal usually is either a light or a tone. With the use of a light as an indicator for heart rate, the patients are asked to control the amount of time the light is on or off. The instructions to them are: "Keep the yellow light on for as long as you can." The patients are not told how they are supposed to be able to do this, but most everyone who has taken part in this experiment has been able to adjust his heart rate so that the light would remain on. The acquisition of self-control skill was personally satisfying to almost everyone who succeeded in controlling their heart rates. These control procedures have been helpful in correcting such cardiac problems as tachycardia and heart flutter.

Headaches

The Menniger Foundation in Topeka, Kansas, has used biofeedback control to help relieve the pain of migraine headaches. Since these headaches have something to do with the main artery for blood in the neck and head, it appears logical that we should look at ways of controlling the flow of blood through those areas. Patients, aided by physicians, learned to bring about changes in their bodies that did lead to less blood being pumped through the arteries and less trouble with migraine headaches. But the patients were not instructed to constrict the walls of the arteries, or lower the blood pressure, or ignore the pain of the headache. Instead, they were instructed to concentrate on making their hands warmer! Temperature sensors were attached to their hands so that they could see their effectiveness in controlling the temperature. In a short time, the patients actually changed the temperature in their hands with the aid of biofeedback and conscious thought. They could never explain just how they did it, but they were able to do it.

While acquiring the ability to raise and lower their hand temperature, the patients lost their migraine headaches. Warming one's hands in a pan of hot water does not eliminate the migraine, but the ability to will one's hands warmer somehow made it possible to discontinue the migraine headache medicines. What has the temperature of the hands got to do with migraine headaches? There has not been a satisfactory explanation yet, but the results show that self-control practices can be used to control headaches caused by the excess flow of blood in arteries.

The potential for humans to self-regulate their hearts in this manner is great. Whenever we are able to substitute self-control with biofeedback for harmful chemical controls, we are going to benefit our bodies.

Asthma

Asthma has been successfully treated with biofeedback machines. The machine is set to respond to calm states in the individual. The patient is asked to imagine those things that will bring on their asthmatic attacks. Sometimes the actual objects are brought near the patient. Whenever the thoughts or objects bring on tension in the individual, the biofeedback machine senses it and reacts by signaling the subject. With training, the patients are taught to remain calm even when the objects cover them. Asthma attacks have been reduced and the need for drugs has been discontinued in some patients who have been taught self-control with biofeedback.

THE RHYTHMS OF THE BRAIN

If you relax yourself and think about nothing specific, then probably you are in a state called "alpha." An alpha state is one of the several brainwave frequencies that have been found to exist in humans. Learning to control brainwaves is supposed to let a person control his mental state. The mental state of alpha is one that reflects itself in a feeling of relaxation. Most of the current research in the control of brainwaves is with alpha rhythms.

Different frequencies of brainwaves correspond to different mental states and emotional feelings. The alpha state has a frequency of 7.5 to 13 cycles per second, and is associated with a mental state of tranquility and relaxation. The theta has a frequency from 3.5 to 7.5 cycles per second, and is associated with the mental state of daydreaming. The theta is noted for periods of creativity and hypnogogic imagery. The delta (0.2 to 3.5 cycles per second) is the usual brainwave for deep sleep. The beta occurs when one is worried, hungry, or fearful.

You can bring about these different brainwaves by engaging

in various activities, or eating or drinking different substances. An alpha state can be entered by lying down and rolling your closed eyes up as far as you can while you are relaxing. Coffee with caffeine will speed up brainwaves, as will the use of amphetamines. This might be the goal if one was interested in the faster frequencies of the beta. Some studies have shown that problem-solving ability is increased with the drinking of coffee. Lower brainwave frequencies occur after alcohol is drunk. These lower frequencies are the delta and the theta (associated with deep sleep).

There has been an emphasis on learning to control the alpha state. The development of the ability to enter the other states may be necessary also. Theta is known for being a possible door to creativity. The control of the other states may be necessary for your exploration of your inner world. Alpha may be good for relaxation, but you may desire other things also. Purchase a biofeedback device that will allow you to select any brainwave frequency.

Problems

The use of biofeedback devices is not without some possible dangers. Improper controls on the heart might lead to heart attacks. The cheaper machines have difficulty in distinguishing between an alpha and a theta or even a muscle twitch. Using a cheap machine and/or conditioning the wrong frequency can reinforce an epileptic brainwave pattern.

Biofeedback unifies the science of behavior. It uses the principles of behavior modification, the techniques of physiology, biochemistry, cybernetics, and electronics to let you control your brain and your body. Given the certain advantages that biofeedback has to offer, it should be considered in your self-control program.

10

Fears and phobias

Fears and phobias are two types of anxiety reactions. Normal fears are common reactions to dangerous situations. These are realistic and serve to protect us from potentially harmful situations. Occasionally, mild and temporary periods of depression and nonspecific fear may be normal. But whenever fears evolve into a long-lasting, unrealistic dread of certain things in the environment, then a phobia is the result. Phobias may be as common as headaches.

Phobias are painful psychological and physiological reactions to stimuli in the world that are not fearful to others. Undergoing a phobic reaction makes one believe that nothing that he does will relieve the painful situations. The physical symptoms of phobias include such things as palpitations of the heart, nausea, diarrhea, shaking, profuse sweating, cold hands, dizziness, and insomnia. Different persons suffer different reactions and different intensities of feeling in their phobic behavior. Usually there is a feeling of one's life being at stake—an internal sense of dread and terror.

The following are recognized phobias: claustrophobia—fear of confined places; acrophobia—fear of heights; noctophobia—fear of the dark; and zoophobia—fear of animals. There is even a fear of "13," which is called triskaidekaphobia. In some manner all these phobias must serve the individual, or they would not be used as behavioral response to the situation in which the person finds himself.

Psychotherapy is normally used to treat individuals who have these unrealistic fears and dreads. The phobia problems are considered to be neuroses, which are not mental illnesses. They are only a learned or conditioned response.

Psychotherapists usually work with patients for long periods of time in order to resolve the phobia problems. Traditional methods of psychotherapy utilize patient-physician interactions that have the doctor spending a lot of time tracing the root of the phobia back to some early period in the patient's life. Supposedly, the present phobia is thought to be the result of some ongoing process that was started by some event in early childhood. The psychotherapist allows the patient to engage in free associations so that the determining factors for the phobias can be discovered and cured. Pressuring the phobic patient is said to lead to defense mechanisms being established that halt the treatment. When this happens, the therapist may resort to powerful drugs to calm the patient.

The overemphasis on internal psychic agents in explaining phobias has restricted the development of workable principles of behavior in the area of phobia treatment. If progress is to occur, there must be a science of treatment that is built upon sound and efficient principles. The current experimental research with behavior modification allows for such applications of procedures that lead to the control of phobic behaviors.

Psychologists now realize that phobias are responses to environmental factors, and these responses are learned. John Watson experimentally induced a phobia in a child by making a frightening noise each time a rabbit was present. After the conditioning, just the sight of the rabbit was enough to cause extreme fear in the child. It is now realized that phobias are learned; therefore learning or conditioning can remove those fears. Present behavior modification psychotherapy may be considered a reeducation process that is used to modify the improper stimulus-response connections present in a phobia. A new, improved response replaces the old dreadful feeling. Basically the relearning process has the patient learning to completely relax, since a person cannot be frightened and relaxed at the same time.

The new form of psychotherapy does not use in-depth biographical analyses to determine the root cause of the phobias. The emphasis is on the acquisition of behavioral changes only. The criticism of this approach is that unless you cure the underlying problem, controlling the resultant symptom is only going to lead to a substitution in the symptom location. This is analogous to reducing the fever of a disease by placing the person in a refrigerator. The question is: "Does behavior-modification therapy of phobias lead to a masking of a more serious problem in patients?"

There is a satisfactory answer to the criticism. In the hundreds of cases of phobias (as well as the many other behavioral problems) that have been treated during the last few years with behavior-modification techniques, there have been no cases of symptom substitution.

If you are contemplating using the techniques to control your phobias, judge the effects of the proposed changes against the possibility of misjudging the cause of the problem. Do not use your time to correct a problem that really does not exist. Suppose that you cut your finger. Would you bandage the finger on your other hand or take an aspirin to stop the bleeding of the injured finger? It is good to be able to control the fears of the mind, but to hide some fears may be dangerous. Would you want to mask your fears of a live rattlesnake?

There have been academic discussions of the effects of operant conditioning. The criticisms have revolved around the aspect of mind control (visions of George Orwell's *1984*) and symptom substitution (the incorrect treatment of a disease). The remainder of this chapter ignores the various criticisms and turns to an analysis of the principles and techniques that have been effective in changing people's behaviors in terms of their reactions to situations producing fears and phobias. Behavior-modification principles applied to the treatment of phobias have been effective in 90 percent of the patients in some cases. This has occurred without years of costly professional treatment. You must make the determination of whether to use the techniques on yourself.

THE DESENSITIZATION OF PHOBIAS

In the last few years a radical change has taken place in the psychological views regarding the nature of and the treatment for fears and phobias. Abnormal fears are not a symptom of some internal illness, but represent the individual's learned method of dealing with the environment. The principles of operant conditioning as developed and used in the area of behavior modification have been especially effective in controlling phobias. The techniques have been used with or without psychoanalytical treatment.

The current success of the treatment method lies with its reliance on the power of the mind to heal those phobias generated by that same mind. It does not look at any unconscious motivations and conflicts, but instead directs its attention to modifying the behavior.

The best known method is "systematic desensitization," which was originally developed by J. Wolpe.[1] The method lacks an underlying theoretical explanation of why it works and it does not identify the causes of phobias, fears, neuroses, or anxiety. What it does do is to quickly and effectively remove a person's fears without causing another problem to emerge.

Wolpe and Lazarus have brought about changes with the use of systematic desensitization of the following phobias: illness, crowds, sex, death, closed places, being watched, heights, storms, among others.[2] Their conclusion, which has been shared by others who use the technique, is that it is not necessary to uncover the patient's unconscious reasons and motivations for phobias in order to successfully control the fears. Also, the use of systematic desensitization does not lead to symptom substitution nor does it change basic attitudes or the patient's personality.

Systematic desensitization means that a person is trained to become less sensitive to the events of the environment. Imagery and the power of the mind are used to confront the feared thing while the person masters the technique of complete relaxation.

The following are the principles on which systematic desensitization is formulated:
1. Relaxation is a more enjoyable state than that of being tense and fearful.
2. The belief in the power of behavior-modification techniques is necessary for effective fear control.
3. The presentation of the feared situation without punishment leads to extinction of the fear response.
4. Fear and relaxation are incompatible behaviors.

Patients are taken through five stages in a systematic desensitization program to remove the effects of a fear or phobia. First, they are taught the methods for achieving complete muscular relaxation. Second, the patients are asked to determine those things that lead to their anxiety reactions and rank them according to the perceived level of intensity of anxiety produced. Third, the patients imagine the situation that is the least frightening and practice their relaxation at the same time. Fourth, once they have been able to think about a fearful situation and remain relaxed, they move to the next higher fear situation. Finally, they reach the actual event, which they confront and attempt to remain relaxed. Note that this is a gradual process that must be practiced daily. The amount of anxiety that relaxation is able to control is small and therefore the differences between levels of anxiety situations should be small.

The desensitization process has as a goal the relaxed confrontation of the most frightening situation as determined by the patient. Relaxation is sometimes taught by hypnosis, which is enhanced by deep breathing, progressive relaxation of the muscles of the entire body, and visualizing calm scenes. But research has shown that relaxation alone is insufficient to remove the effects of the phobia.[3] The process of confronting different levels of the hierarchy of the fear is responsible for reducing the phobic behavior.

Anxiety can be measured with instruments. Biofeedback machines can be adapted to record changes in a person's blood pressure, heart rates, galvanic skin responses (to determine the amount of perspiration), and respiration rates. Whenever excessive physiological reactions occur in response to the imagined phobic situation, muscle relaxation can be attempted. The feedback of the body responses can be used to measure objectively how effective the relaxation techniques are in controlling the situation. This is systematic desensitization with biofeedback.

Normally it takes from eight to twelve weeks to take a person through the desensitization process until he reaches the final, most fearful situation. The treatments last from half an hour to two hours a day. The techniques have been taught to patients for home use after the relaxation procedures have been taught. Treatment at home takes an additional two to three weeks over what it takes with the help of a therapist. This is probably due to having to acquire some of the skills through trial and error learning.

Systematic desensitization works. It controls phobic behavior in a relatively short time (as compared with psychoanalytical methods). And the effects of the procedures seem to be permanent. In one study, 90 percent of those treated for the elimination of their fear of speaking in front of groups of people went on to excel in academic performance; whereas, only 60 percent of a nontreated control group were able to do the same things.[4] Wolpe reported that there was less than a 2-percent relapse rate for the patients that he treated with systematic desensitization procedures. Oher research studies show that subjects that were conditioned with desensitization therapy showed a greater reduction in reducing their fears of phobic situations than did control groups receiving no treatment. Studies done six months and a year after treatment show that the previous patients have actually improved on their earlier desensitization with self-control.

THE PATIENT AS THE THERAPIST

A patient cures his own fears and phobias. The external factor, the professional therapist, is able to help the person to reach his desired goal more efficiently, but the therapist is never able to force a behavioral change where one is not wanted. The person that has a phobia cannot be cured until he has tried a new behavior on his own and been met with reinforcement rather than punishment. Curing a phobia requires the patient's active help. The success of systematic desensitization must depend upon the trust the patient has in the techniques. Resistance in any manner to change will destroy the effectiveness of the procedures. The major purpose of an external therapist is to provide assurances and motivation until personal satisfaction with the progress of the program becomes self-motivating.

The use of professional help in psychotherapy can usually be dispensed with if the patient can supply the necessary self-control to practice the technique. In the final analysis, emotional changes in a patient are brought about by psychiatrists who have been allowed to practice by the patient. The patient becomes his own therapist.

The self-control of fear and phobic behaviors requires that you recognize the functional relationship that exists between the mind and the body, and the effect that one has on the other. To prevent fear of the environment, you should have respect for your body and confidence in your ability to control yourself. Once you witness your ability to master various levels of a fear hierarchy, you will notice that you have increased confidence in yourself and your ability to handle other fearful situations. Self-confidence grows with practice.

MacClean and Graff have developed a self-control approach to controlling your phobias.[5] They suggest that you must confront the fear and avoid escaping from the feared situation. Follow the techniques of systematic desensitization until you are able to put yourself into the most feared situation without becoming tense. You must practice relaxation at each step in the hierarchy. Your full attention to the fear and to the fear situation is required if the technique is to work. Images of the situation work over a period of time, but the actual situation will bring forth quicker results.

Take your time. Decide what it is that you are actually

afraid of and what the environmental factors are that are responsible for those fears. Look at the incremental things that lead up to the final fearful situation. Rank these events. Then start with the lowest anxiety-producing event and consciously practice relaxation until it no longer produces tenseness in you. Work your way up the fear hierarchy.

The process may be enhanced with the aid of someone that you can pattern your responses after. Seeing another person handling a snake without suffering any of your fear reactions is effective in reducing your phobias about snakes. Once again the approach must be gradual. It does no good for that person to throw the snake toward you in the hope that you will see how illogical your fear is. Gradually work your way toward just looking at the snake that someone else is holding—practicing your relaxation at the same time. Over a period of several weeks you will be able to hold the snake without suffering any anxiety, tenseness, or phobic reactions.

Subjects who have shown great fear in talking to groups of people have been able to reduce their anxieties substantially and practice desensitization on themselves with the use of recorded self-instructions containing commands to relax and imagine calm scenes. The subjects imagined increasingly more demanding speaking situations and listened to and obeyed the self-command on the recorder.[6]

The importance of the fear hierarchy must be kept in mind. Once a weak stimulus is unable to elicit tenseness or anxiety, a more threatening situation must be presented and adjusted to. The events in the hierarchy must be directly related to the final most fearful event. The distance between each of the steps must be kept small because the effectiveness of relaxation to conquer larger anxiety reactions is not good. If you attempt to reduce a phobia in one big move, you will actually increase your tension in response to that situation. The key is to develop the ability to remain relaxed and calm at all times. The chapter on relaxation methods and self-hypnosis will present ways in which you can learn to be relaxed even when confronted with stressful situations.

FEAR OF FLYING

The following is an account of my personal systematic desensitization of a flying phobia. I am not sure what my actual fears could be called. A fear of heights would be called acrophobia, but I did not feel afraid on the top of skyscrapers. I do not believe that I had a death phobia. It might be that I just had a fear of being in an airplane that was flying. What the name of the fear was does not really matter. The important factor to me was how to control the horrible symptoms of my phobic reactions while flying.

It did not seem to cause me any stress to be in an airplane that was on the ground, but as soon as the wheels left the ground I became totally afraid of the situation. Every muscle became tense. My stomach became violently upset. I would begin to sweat profusely. My heart felt as though it had speeded up by ten times its normal rate. Gradually over the span of an hour or two of a flight I would calm down a little, but if there was any turbulence I would suffer the entire trip. Approaches to landing had to be the worst fear that I have ever faced. I got so tense at times that my muscles would hurt for days afterward. I could not breathe during the last thirty seconds just before touchdown. As soon as the wheels touched the pavement, I was normal once again.

I realized that the phobia I had was not realistic. But telling myself just before a landing that I was acting irrationally did not calm me.

I attempted to solve the phobia by determining my chances for having an accident while flying. I knew that I had no fears about driving an automobile even though there are 50 thousand people a year killed while driving a car. I did not fear choking to death on the food that I ate even though I found out that nearly 4,000 people a year die from choking to death on their food. It seemed logical to me that since only one or two hundred people die in scheduled airline crashes I stood a better chance statistically in an airplane than in a car. In fact, it is twenty-five times safer to fly than to drive. Why fear flying? I had a phobia.

I had a dread of flying that was unrealistic and not supported by the facts. My fear existed as a figment of my vivid imagination.

I finally decided to look at the alternatives that were available to me regarding the fear of flying. I had three choices. I could avoid flying at all costs, therefore never having to face the anxiety situation. I discarded this choice as unreasonable in today's society. I could go on forcing myself to fly and hating every minute of the flights. I decided that I would rather enjoy life; therefore, I had to find a way to conquer my phobia. I could fly continually afraid or conquer the fear.

I decided to control my fear of flying by establishing a self-control program using the principles of behavior modification, especially the techniques of systematic desensitization. I developed my own personal self-improvement program. I did not use a practicing psychologist or professional therapist. I knew what my final goal was to be—to remain calm during a flight in an airplane, especially the landings. This goal presented somewhat of a problem in terms of developing a hierarchy of increasingly frightening situations. I did not become afraid until after the plane left the ground. Thinking about the flight beforehand, going up to the plane, or anything else that might be useful in developing a hierarchy was missing.

I decided after a period of thinking about the subject that a major contributor to my fear of flying was the feeling of powerlessness. I believe that the key to self-control of fears and phobias is with the feeling that one has whether or not he can cope with a particular situation. Flying in a scheduled airline, passively sitting in the passenger section, and not contributing anything to the flight is not an ideal way to actively confront one's fears. Passivity generates anxieties. I needed some method that would allow me to take over some of the decisions about flying. If I was going to get over the fear, I decided that I must take an active part in a flying situation. I must learn to fly solo.

A major contributor to my ongoing fear of flying was *not* flying. My irrational fears about flying would never diminish unless I behaved in such a way as to put myself into active flying situations. I could have gotten through many years without getting into an airplane. In this manner I would not have that irrational fear; at least it would not be making me feel miserable.

I made the decision to enroll in one of the best flight schools in the United States. The fact that it was part of the University of North Dakota made me feel more confident in the program. I applied myself to learning all about private aircraft. Ground school is a good way to develop a hierarchy. You gradually approach the flying situation only after you have acquired a certain amount of basic knowledge. The time I spent studying basic aerodynamics and flying procedures helped me to develop my powers of imagination. By practicing relaxation and visualizing flying situations at the same time, I was able to remain calm in increasingly more stressful situations.

During the time I was spending at ground school I was looking for a flight instructor. The person that I was looking for had to have certain characteristics or I would not be able to have any faith in his ability to control the flying situations completely. I needed someone who I felt could handle any flying situation there was, while at the same time not having to prove to me that he could. I needed a person of stable flying characteristics, not one who would turn the plane upside down suddenly and then say to me, "See how well this plane flies? You do not have any reason to be scared."

I found a flight instructor who knew how to fly so well he never had to try and prove it to me by any exotic maneuver. The instructor who I selected knew the rules and regulations of flying. He knew the aircraft characteristics and limitations. And, most importantly, he had good judgment and considerable patience.

I modified my original goal somewhat. I decided that I needed to be able to get my private pilot's license. The reason for this was in order to get the license one had to be able to fly solo for several hundred miles. The ability to fly rested solely with me. If I let fear render me completely immovable, I knew that I could never land the plane. Since I would be alone I could not let this happen. Also, in order to get a license you had to go through a series of increasingly more difficult and more stressful flight situations.

Over a period of several months a student is expected to master such things as slow flight, turns around a fixed point, cross-country flights, and the stall. Practicing the stall was the most horrible experience of my life. It is done by slowly pulling the nose of the aircraft up. You keep this up until the aircraft loses so much airspeed that the lift on the wings is insufficient to fly. When an airplane stalls, it falls. To pass the flying test at the end of the program a student is expected to engage in a stall, and, of course, to recover from it. My problem with learning to stall an airplane was getting into the situation. I did not have any difficulty recovering from the situation of an airplane falling to the ground. I reacted immediately with the correct responses to bring the airplane out of the fall. During the initial learning of the stall procedures, I had my instructor with me, ready at all times to correct any of my errors.

Gradually over the period of time that I was learning to fly, I developed more confidence in my abilities to handle flying situations. When the day of my first solo flight came, I was frightened. Once I got off the ground and knew that I could not turn to anyone to get me down, I relied on my confidence in my flying abilities to relax my fears.

Being alone to confront one's phobias does not always work to keep one relaxed. Once while I was visiting a control tower, a student pilot became so frightened that he was unable to land the airplane. The student's instructor had to talk the person back to the ground. The eventual landing was uneventful, but I am sure the fear that resulted from the person's not being able to control the situation only increased whatever fears he already had. In my judgment the student was not ready to fly by himself. The situation was too stressful for relaxation methods to counteract the fears.

Through a process of gradual confrontations with phobic stimuli, I was able to remain calm during an entire flight. The final stage was when I was able to land the airplane by myself and remain calm.

A fear of flying can be controlled just like any other phobia. Make a list of the fears associated with flying. These may be the takeoffs or the landings, fears of the height, being closed in, and so on. Rank these fears into order of increasing fears. Visualize each stage while practicing relaxation. Once that stage has been met, move on to the next. Confront the things that you fear. Do so gradually. And practice the relaxation procedures. Do not attempt to overwhelm the anxiety by taking too large a step up the hierarchy. Return to those levels where you can handle the anxiety by relaxing. Take trips in airplanes with individuals that you admire. Do not just sit in an airplane and let the fear surround you. Do something else to take your mind off the event. Learn to fly yourself. I am now proud and pleased with my ability to control myself in situations that I previously feared.

11

Relaxation and self-hypnosis

The ability to relax is the key to reducing the effects of stress. A person who can relax is able to reduce tension and headaches, lower blood pressure, and do many other things. Self-hypnosis opens the door to improved methods of concentration, better learning, and the greater ability to develop effective self-control over other activities. Relaxation and self-hypnosis are closely allied, in that the development of one helps to develop the other. There is little well-documented research with the effects of relaxation and self-hypnosis. It is generally accepted that both methods allow an individual to adapt easily to environmental changes and requirements. Both techniques are useful to know and apply in self-control procedures.

The differences between self-hypnosis and self-relaxation are few. In fact, to achieve a hypnotic state the hypnotist attempts to place the subject into a state of deepening relaxation. Research shows that concentration is the biggest factor in acquiring deep relaxation or hypnosis. This chapter looks at the aspects of relaxation, including the methods of relaxing; and self-hypnosis is explored in terms of how to achieve it for self-control.

SELF-RELAXATION

There is some difficulty in establishing a goal that is structured in terms of relaxation. The objective measurement of what it means to be relaxed is not at all precise. The principle of behavior modification suggests that self-control is obtainable whenever there is a behavior that can be controlled and measured. How do you know when you are relaxed? Is there a way to determine if the state is as good as you can get it? Are you relaxed all the way? Relaxation is the result of a technique stressing and then relaxing the muscles of the body. The state of being relaxed is measured internally by one's assessment of the difference between effort and noneffort. Working hard for thirty minutes doing exercises, followed by a period of doing nothing physical, will result in a feeling in the body of being relaxed. For example, tighten your fist as hard as you can and hold it for thirty seconds. Let the hand become limp. Notice the difference in feeling. The ability to determine whether or not you are relaxed depends upon your ability to detect the degree of difference between a tense state and normal tonus in the body.

Achieving relaxation requires daily practice. Five or ten minutes every day spent practicing the techniques of bodily relaxation will be sufficient. As the procedures become a part of your behaviors, you will notice that you start to use them to keep you relaxed during stressful situations. This is where the value of relaxation comes to you.

An internal feeling of calmness and serenity can be measured with the aid of the electronic devices that were discussed earlier. In fact, it might be worthwhile to establish your goals for relaxation in terms of the objective measurement of electronically monitored physiological functions. You may state your goals in terms of lower blood pressure, reduced muscular tension, fewer heartbeats, or some other measure. The good thing about using these devices to control your relaxation states is that you get immediate feedback.

Tensions make themselves apparent by your behaviors. People who are tense will tap their feet, chew on pencils or their fingers, grind their teeth, talk to themselves, and chain-smoke. Tension needs an outlet and these physical activities allow some of the pressures to be reduced. Tensions can be worked out of the body. A regular program of hard exercises will help you to become relaxed. The effects of a regular program of physical activities will be apparent for a long time after they have been finished.

Yoga exercises are an ideal method to help you to develop relaxation because they are formulated so that you first stretch your muscles, then let go, and this produces the calm state. The use of the electronic biofeedback devices can do about the same thing as physical exertion, but in only twenty minutes.

Relaxation is nothing but a learned technique. Since we express our feelings and emotions through our muscles, we can affect the mental state by our activities.

Relaxation can be achieved by a constant, daily program that involves physical exercise, followed by a period of total rest, and deep breathing. At first it is best to practice relaxation control in an isolated part of the house. You need a place where you can lie down and not be distracted. If you have an alpha machine that will help you to know when you are in the relaxed state where the alpha rhythms of the brain predominate, this will allow you to achieve the deepest and also the quickest state of relaxation.

Close your eyes and talk yourself into a state of being totally relaxed. There are commercially available recordings that talk you into relaxed states. You may want to invest some money in one of these to help you achieve the desired state. Tell yourself that you are going to relax all your muscles. Start with those in your neck.

Say to yourself: "The muscles in my neck are becoming very relaxed. They have no tension in them at all." Let them be as loose as you can. Breathe deeply. "My arms are becoming very loose, and the muscles are getting more and more relaxed." Devise your own statements. Approach the relaxation state in gradual stages. The achievement of relaxation is worth the trouble that you put into it. The best time to learn the self-control of relaxaion is at your normal bedtime. It is easier to learn to relax when you are tired. Once you have mastered the ability to enter a relaxed state at will, you can broaden the places where you are able to relax yourself.

Self-Hypnosis

You can use self-hypnosis to reach your subconscious mind. Self-hypnosis is a technique that is easy to acquire. The problem with attempting to use self-hypnosis is that the effects are hard to measure and there is a tendency to stop practicing the technique after only a short while. Once again the value of a goal, a personal contract, and a schedule becomes readily apparent. If you decide to establish a self-hypnosis program, utilize the principles of behavior modification to make sure that you stay with your plans.

Self-hypnosis can be structured to fit the needs of your self-improvement program. The benefits of using self-hypnosis should be generalized, nonspecific factors. People who have developed their abilities to use self-hypnosis have had the following improvements in themselves: improvements in their ability to concentrate, better learning, more self-confidence, reduction in fears and phobias, creativity, and better self-control.

The fastest method for achieving self-control is to be hypnotized by some professional in the field and be given a posthypnotic suggestion that will allow you to control your own hypnotic states. But professional help may not be available to you. One way of achieving self-hypnosis without being hypnotized by another person is to put the hypnotic instructions onto a tape and then play these suggestions back to yourself. There are recorded messages commercially available that will make the task of achieving self-hypnosis remarkably easy.

Some mechanical devices that may be used to achieve self-hypnosis are: any object that you can direct or fix your gaze upon, the flame of a candle, a metronome, a glass ball, a dangling object such as a watch at the end of a chain. These mechanical devices only help when used in a concentrated effort. They never guarantee success. Actually a spot on the wall is all you need to achieve self-hypnosis. Once you have acquired the ability to enter a hypnotic state with the aid of some device, it becomes easier to condition yourself to respond to an image that you have in your mind. A key thought or concept may be all that is needed for you to put yourself into a relaxed and self-hypnotic state.

This will come if you apply on a daily basis the practice that is required.

Concentration

You must develop the ability to concentrate if you are to acquire self-hypnosis. Being relaxed also means that you must concentrate on something other than your tensions and pressures. Many individuals have found that they can ignore the turmoil that is going on around them if they allow themselves to concentrate on something. Riders of subways or buses can read while considerable activity is going on, but they still are able to get off at the right stop. Their ability to concentrate on a book, a crossword puzzle, or a daydream allows them to ignore potentially stressful situations.

To concentrate on reading, writing, or studying in a noisy environment is difficult. To establish an environment conducive to concentration it may be necessary to do some restructuring. If your noisy television is distracting you from your studying, you can always sell it or disconnect it. If it is your neighbor's television, you may have to find a way to work around the distraction. You might want to buy some earplugs or work at times when the distractions are at a minimum. Another technique for noise-proofing your environment is to purchase a white-noise generator. An inexpensive electric fan does a good job of masking distracting noises. Buy a loud fan. You can always vary its intensity by placing it nearer or farther away from you. I have used the fan to help me concentrate and also to make it easier to go to sleep at night. There are devices on the market now that sound like slowly falling raindrops or the sound of the surf. These result in the same thing as a white-noise generator—they mask extraneous and distracting noises.

Concentration also depends on your motivation. If the pressure of a task is great, then you are more or less forced into concentration to accomplish the task. This is why placing yourself on a schedule is effective in generating concentration. Concentration is an ability that develops your self-control through daily practice. Write down your goal of achieving the ability to concentrate. Arrange your environmental contingencies for concentration. Establish a schedule of daily commitments to concentration. It will not be long before you are able to relax and to concentrate upon a single item at will.

I have developed the following circle-concept to aid in concentration. It starts out by being a drawing of a circle with some lines through it, but with continued efforts the device becomes a mental image to aid in concentrating and self-hypnosis.

The subconscious concentration circle is a device that I have developed which will allow you to communicate directly with your inner mind. The Chevreul Pendulum method for hypnosis has been used for many years. Hypnotists, magicians, and mystics attach a weight to a string and hold it over a circle. As a person concentrates, the weight traces a path over the circle. The movement is directed by the person's subconscious mind. The Chevreul Pendulum serves to focus one's attention.

I have adapted this idea of forcing one's concentration onto a circle by constructing a circle that has been divided into quadrants. The following drawing represents a device that I have been using with great effectiveness to reach my subconscious mind. My circle has allowed me to develop my powers of self-hypnosis to a great extent.

You can construct a device like mine to develop your powers of concentration. A compass, ruler, and some India ink will be needed. Carefully ink in the circle. Take as long as you need to construct a perfect circle. I found that the image of the circle stayed with me after I had experimented with several different sizes of circles. I divided the circle into quadrants by inking in two lines. I experimented with different figures in two of the quadrants. I finally decided on using the small darkened circle and the darkened ellipse that are shown in the drawing. Once you have a perfect circle, concentrate on it daily for a week or so until it forms a vivid image in your mind. You should be able to close your eyes and mentally see the figure. Your ability to concentrate and to present mental suggestions to yourself will depend upon your success in forming a clear mental picture of the circle and its component parts.

The circle can be used to develop your powers of concentra-

Relaxation and self-hypnosis 111

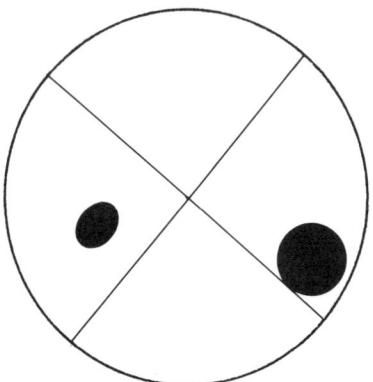

FIGURE 1. THE SUBCONSCIOUS CONCENTRATION CIRCLE

tion. Start your relaxation process. Relax your muscles and clear stressful thoughts from your conscious mind. Think relaxing thoughts. Then visualize the circle as clearly as you can. Look at the actual drawing if you find yourself unable to develop a clear mental picture. With the imagination that you have, trace the circle's circumference. Then mentally go along the two straight lines. Next, visualize the dark-black, solid circle that is in one of the quadrants of the larger circle. Once you "see" these parts of your concentration circle, imagine the ellipse. (Your experimentation may lead you to use other forms than circles or ellipses in your concentration circle.) Now picture the complete circle with all its component parts. Refer to the drawing anytime you feel that you are losing any part of the mental image.

Now that you have relaxed and can form a mental image of the concentration circle, it is time to learn the method of sequential numbering. In the upper quadrant of Figure 2 you will see the number "10". Visualize in your mind that number, while at the same time keeping the entire circle and its parts in clear detail in your mind. Keep referring to the circle that you have drawn and imagine it with the "10" in one of the empty quadrants. You started with a drawing of a circle that enclosed two straight lines and two solid figures. Now you are mentally writing upon that circle a "10." Mentally see the circle with the number in it. This will force you to concentrate.

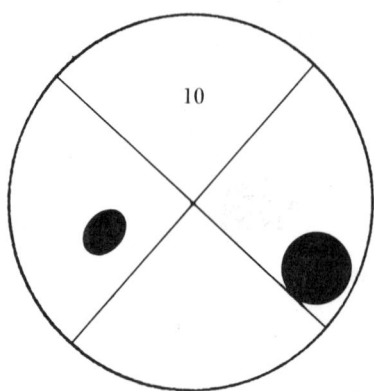

FIGURE 2. NUMBERING THE CONCENTRATION CIRCLE

Next, mentally count backward from ten and at the same time put the corresponding number into the proper quadrant. As you picture the number "9" it should appear in the quadrant of your concentration circle. Then do the same for all the numbers till you get to "1." When you mentally reach "1" with your backward counting procedure, start over again with "10." Do this three or four times every day for a week and your powers of concentration will improve significantly. It will not take long before you are able to visualize your concentration circle in all kinds of situations.

With the ability to form the complete circle and to imagine the series of numbers in one of the quadrants, you can now begin to establish the procedure for reaching your subconscious. Starting with "10" in one of the quadrants, form a mental message

Relaxation and self-hypnosis   113

in the remaining blank quadrant of your concentration circle. Your mental picture then can be counted down, just as you did in practicing your ability to concentrate. Figure 3 shows how the phrase "I feel good" can be placed into the circle and counted backward with. The idea of counting backward while visualizing a positive message is to deepen your level of concentration.

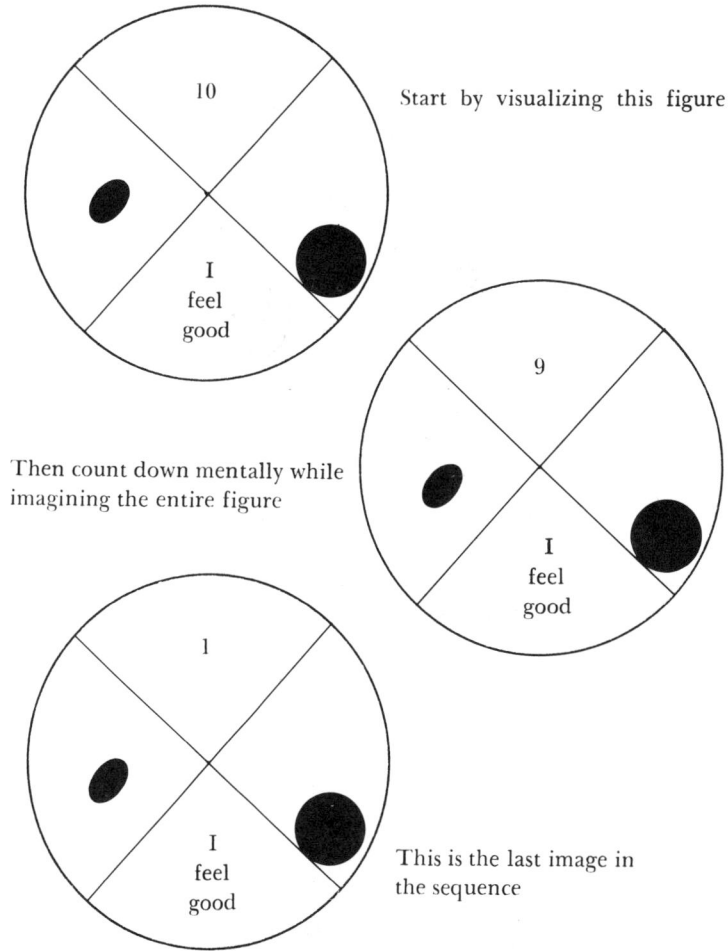

Start by visualizing this figure

Then count down mentally while imagining the entire figure

This is the last image in the sequence

FIGURE 3.   WRITING THE MENTAL MESSAGE

Continue visualizing the circle, its parts, the sequence of numbers, and the phrase. With each of the numbers visualize your positive phrase to your subconscious. Practice this method of reaching your subconscious after you go to bed at night. You will usually fall asleep before reaching the number "1" for the second time. If not, start over with "10," count backward in your mind, keep visualizing the message, and soon you will be sound asleep with the instructions to yourself written in your mind.

Keep your instructions to yourself short, positive, and realistic. Do not expect complete results in one night. A possible way to reinforce your instructions would be to tape them and play them to yourself as you go to sleep. You could attach a timer which would cut the machine off after an hour or so of repeating the message to you.

Outline of the Method

1. Construct the circle and its components with great care. Experiment with several until you find one that seems to "fit."

2. Develop your ability to picture the circle in your mind.

3. Learn to visualize in your mind the sequence of numbers in the quadrants. Picture "10," "9," and so on until you reach "1."

4. Keep this up until you develop good powers of concentration.

5. Imagine a short, positive phrase in the remaining empty quadrant.

6. Practice this procedure every night without fail for at least one week before you expect to feel any of the desired changes in yourself.

The ability of hypnotism to implant subtle messages in the subconscious mind is supported by the experimental evidence and research findings. A hypnotically induced state in which messages are delivered can improve your ability to control yourself. Your resolve to follow your own prescribed course of action will be enhanced by self-hypnosis.

There are some good reasons why you should develop the powers of concentration and the ability to enter into self-hypnotic states. The hypnotic state is noted for its responsiveness to many kinds of suggestions. The conditioned response characterized by hypnosis is never lost.

The preceding self-hypnotic procedure allows you to write messages to your subconscious on a mental blackboard. The continual intelligent use of this technique offers you a lot in terms of concentration, relaxation, self-control, and self-improvement. The concentration circle presents conditioning statements to your subconscious mind.

Do not attempt to force results with the procedure. Do not expect too much. It can never repair what is ruined. Merely repeating some statement over and over will not bring about changes. We can alter only those things that we make a substantial conscious effort to. Desire and concerted effort are the real keys to self-improvement.

Calculus by Self-Hypnosis

The following is an example of how I used the concentration circle to greatly improve my ability to learn differential and integral calculus. While attending school I took a mathematics course that I needed to graduate. I went to class regularly, listened to the lecturer, and made a deliberate effort to work all the assigned problems. But try as I would, my understanding of the problems was limited. I just did not know how to solve a calculus problem. The further along I got into the semester, the more anxiety I felt regarding the calculus course. About midway through the course I became anxious whenever I tried to sit down and work a homework problem. As a result, I let the work and the study of the material slip by me. This compounded my anxiety. When the week of finals arrived I was terrified. I either had to make sense out of calculus or I would definitely flunk the final and not graduate from college.

I analyzed my situation. Each time I tried to study I would get so nervous that any excuse would be used to put off the study of calculus. If I was to learn the subject, I must spend some amount of time reading about it. I made myself a behavior modification program of study. I scheduled myself to spend three hours a day for a week to do nothing but read and study that one subject. Each day that I put in the required number of hours I allowed myself a positive reinforcement. Any day that I did not spend three hours with calculus I allowed myself no positive reinforcements.

The control of my anxiety was another matter. I needed to be relaxed in order to let my subconscious mind sort through the concepts of calculus. After spending the three hours of each day in active study of calculus, I would go to bed at night just after a brief review of all that I had learned up to that point. Each night I would use my concentration circle to relax myself. In addition to the relaxation I gave myself the following message: "I will understand calculus." This message I imagined in one of the circle's quadrants. Each night I would count down from ten to one. Sometimes it took four or five times of going through the sequence in order for me to fall off to sleep. But whenever I finally did get to sleep, I would have relaxed dreams about that day's study of calculus.

Forty-eight hours before my final I started a marathon study of calculus. For a straight fifteen hours I read, worked all the problems that I could, talked to other students in my calculus class, and got help in those areas that were giving me the most trouble. Then I went to sleep for about ten hours after I went through my conditioning practice with the concentration circle. I remember that the last thought on my conscious mind as I drifted into sleep was: "I will understand calculus."

I had a dream that night. I dreamed that I was looking at a huge book and a hand was turning the pages of the book slowly so that I could fully read each page. The book was a calculus book and I was understanding every thing that was written in it. I awoke the next day feeling greatly relieved in the knowledge that I now understood calculus. I was able to go into the final feeling confident in my ability to handle the situation fully. Also, knowing that I understood the principles and concepts of calculus made it quite easy to relax myself even though I faced a stressful situation. I made an "A" on the final and graduated from college.

The grade that I made on the exam was not a gift, nor was it the result of some mystical, hypnotic experience. It came about because I spent a number of hours of concentrated effort in studying the material. Something did not enter my subconscious that night and pour the information into my head. I had to do a lot of hard work in order to get the information into my brain. Even though I did not understand calculus until the night before my exam, I still attended class and tried to understand the material. The one problem that kept me from arriving at my level of understanding earlier was the severe anxiety that I felt. To learn one must be partially relaxed. Calmness is one state that makes learning easier. I was tense because I did not understand the solutions to the calculus problems, but at the same time I could not study because I became too tense. The secret was to learn to relax and to use my periods of sleep to sort through the material that I had read and studied during the day.

Sleep Learning

Messages can be prerecorded and played to yourself at night while you sleep. Some believe that this technique is effective in conditioning one's attitudes and behavior. Research has shown that it is possible to change behavior through sleep learning, but only when certain conditions are met.

During deep sleep little outside learning is acquired. The most effective time for messages to reach the subconscious is the fifteen to thirty minutes just before you enter deep sleep. Thus a message is more likely to reach your subconscious if it is presented as you are going to sleep. Research shows that people report dreaming about their last thought or something that was on their minds just before sleeping.

The concentration circle presented earlier is a good method for reaching the subconscious mind with messages and commands. Before you retire each night, mentally picture the concentration circle and a message written upon it. To increase the learning effects, prerecord a message that will automatically turn on and off at different times during the night. Whenever a mental image has been formed and reinforced with verbal commands, learning abilities are enhanced. After you repeat your conditioning suggestions to yourself and then go to sleep, the additional repetition of the message from the recording will improve your control of your subconscious.

Much thinking is done subconsciously. Recordings of a sleeping brain show that it is receptive and alert. The kinds of material that it responds to while in a sleeping condition are different from that of a waking condition, but it does respond to generalized sorts of inputs. People that have been sprinkled with water while they sleep report dreaming of rain.

Factual learning during sleep does not seem to occur. It may be possible to reach the sleeping brain with nonspecific instructions. The best time may be just before deep sleep. These drowsy states are susceptible to suggestions that may modify attitudes and pave the way for more effective self-control.

Self-control of your sleeping problems can be helped with some of the principles of behavior modification. Sleeping problems may be controlled by arranging the right environmental contingencies. If you find yourself unable to sleep after lying down, do not lie there in the bed and toss and turn for hours. Get up and go to another part of the house and do something else. A common reason for not sleeping is anxiety. The practice of relaxation methods is helpful in establishing a stimulus for sleep.

A method for achieving sleep is to count something in your mind. Some people count sheep, but a slightly different version of this classic approach is to count behaviorally modified "sheep." Purchase a plastic counter and take it to bed with you. Mentally say to yourself "one-thousand-and-one," "one-thousand-and-two," and so on until you reach "one-thousand-and-ten." Press the counter once. Then start over with the mental numbering sequence. A person having real difficulty falling asleep may have one hundred clicks on the counter before he falls asleep. When you awake each morning, record the number from the counter onto the graph that you are keeping to determine how long it takes you to get to sleep. Your goal may be to be able to fall asleep within "one" on your counter.

There are several helpful hints for achieving sleep. Drinking warm milk, doing some exercises, making sure that you are tired before lying down to sleep, practicing techniques for relaxation, removing aversive stimuli, and arranging the sleep environment are some of the ways people get to sleep.

A recent experimental method for inducing sleep is called the electrosone.[1] The electric sleep that is produced by the electrosone results from the central nervous system being retarded in its electrical activity. The technique is experimental but could prove helpful to chronic insomniacs.

CONCLUSIONS

This chapter looks at two important factors that will expand your ability to control yourself and at the same time enjoy life more. Relaxation is something that is relatively easy to acquire. The problem with learning relaxation, as with so many other self-improvement activities, is that it requires daily practice. Once a person can relax himself on command, it is not too difficult to acquire the ability to enter into self-hypnotic states. Self-hypnosis is an ideal way of presenting generalized suggestions to your subconscious. Consistent practice of the relaxation and self-hypnotic techniques will let you develop great powers of self-control. It will be a milestone in your life when you are able to gain complete control of your subconscious mind.

12

Control your creativity

Creativity is something that can be nurtured. It cannot be created in you, but the conditions necessary for its occurrence can be self-controlled. The assumption is made that if you possess any creativity but have not been able to express it, the problem must be the result of an unfavorable environment for creative expression. The purpose of this chapter is to show you how to apply the principles of behavior modification for the control of your creativity.

CREATIVE THINKING

Creativity is a mental process that leads to unique assessments of things that exist in the world around us. Your ability to think creatively about your environment plus active implementation will lead you to the achievement of self-improvement. Creative thinking is the same as creative problem solving. If you are able to see the solutions to the problems that others miss, you will become a truly creative thinker. The abilities to create solutions to problems can be achieved through skills and practice. Both of these ingredients can be self-arranged so as to lead one to creative thinking. Thinking creatively is a mixture of pragmatic approaches, some imagination, and much hard work. A practical or pragmatic approach to creativity requires the application of routine drills to the intuitive problem. The resulting art of a painter comes from a period of training and deliberate hard work that is mixed with the artist's natural creative abilities. A writer's creativity comes from the skills of learned abilities with words, language, grammar, and the experiences of living. The hard work in applying the skills and techniques to problems leads to creative thinking.

Creativity is a unique arrangement of things that have been around for a while. Creativity is the putting things together in ways that have not been tried before. Creativity is your way of responding to the world around you. Your ability to be creative depends to a great extent on your ability to concentrate and to imagine new relationships among things. Some attributes of creative people are: sensitivity, self-confidence, recognition of problems, humor, and a high degree of self-control. We all possess these attributes in varying amounts. Some can be improved upon by conscious efforts and following techniques of behavior modification. Self-control is but one of the personal factors that can be self-improved through the various principles and procedures that have been presented throughout this book.

The remainder of this chapter presents a self-development program for creativity.

THE DEVELOPMENT AND CONTROL OF CREATIVITY

Creativity is a process that can be controlled with the principles available from behavior modification. Your environment has much to do with the overt expression of creative acts. Since we have seen that it is possible to control yourself by arranging your environment, it should also be possible to develop creative behaviors through the proper contingencies. Although creativity may be present in you, it does not suddenly appear without a period of active effort. The flow of creativity is greatly enhanced by the self-application of various ideational techniques.

An Environment for Creativity

Creativity is your way of interacting in a meaningful way with your environment. Your creativity, or lack of it, is a product of the environment—good or bad—that you find yourself in.

A bad environment will inhibit your cognitive freedom and stifle your creativity. The modern world offers us too little chance to express ourselves in imaginative ways. The drudgery of menial jobs does not present us with the stimulating environment that is necessary if our creativity is to emerge.

One of the problems with the environment is that it inhibits creative thought. It does this by presenting too many alternatives that offer immediate gratification. Instead of spending time thinking about problems and searching for unique solutions to them, we can put these things out of our minds by turning on the television set, going to the movie, or turning off the world by using alcoholic beverages. Creativity is restricted by the great profusion of stimuli that compete for our thoughts. Since the world is so complex and has so many things that pull our attentions in different directions, it is difficult to create. Creative thinking and problem solving require an environment that is relatively free of distractions.

You may be able to schedule creative endeavors around the distractions of the world. The arrangement of time for reflection should be scheduled so that you can have twenty to thirty minutes for concentration throughout different periods of the day. This procedure is only second-best to devoting all your time to creativity.

Think tanks are environments where individuals can apply their thinking about problems without having to face the problems of distracting environmental stimuli. Creativity is a process that can be developed and controlled by the establishment of the proper conditions in the environment. The stimulus situation, the environment, can modify, maintain, and reinforce your innate creative abilities. Interacting with people who are open to new ideas is one way of sparking creativity. Another way is to arrange for a calm, serene place where your subconscious can freely interact with your overt actions to discover new arrangements for things. You must arrange your environment so that it becomes the think tank for your creativity.

You might consider setting aside an area of your house where you will never be disturbed while you think creatively.

Set up a small table with paper and pencil on it. Remove distractions from around the desk. Arrange an environment where the stimulus conditions are so structured and reduced in complexity that thinking is more likely to result. Establish the contingencies for creative thinking. Decide on what reinforcements you are going to give for the desired behaviors. Go into the room or area at specified times during the day. Either stay for certain intervals of time or until you have generated some specified number of ideas.

Your personal experiences in life also shape your ability to express yourself creatively. Do not hide behind the walls of your home and hope that your creativity will somehow be stimulated. Get out and experience life. Meet new people. See new places. Attend night school. Volunteer for some civic activities. Ask more questions of the people you meet. Expand your world. Search for some challenges to your abilities.

Being Creative Is Work

It requires a lot of hard work at the conscious level before we experience creative thought. It seems that conscious activity precedes unconscious creativity. There are many reports of individuals who have had difficult problems to solve. Having worked on the solutions to the problems for hours without success, these individuals quit working on the problem and found something else to do. Some went to bed, others took long walks. A strange thing occurs—after you have worked for great lengths on a problem, the solution suddenly appears from the subconscious mind. Effort followed by nonforced activity may lead to creative insights.

I have taken a nap after spending hours of conscious efforts on a particular problem. After the nap I would remember dreaming about the solutions to that problem.

Artists speak of letting their efforts simmer for a time before they feel that they are ready to create something.

The basic factors necessary for creativity to occur have been suggested by Henri Poincaré in "Mathematical Creation" and Stephen Spender in "The Making of a Poem."[1] Poincaré and

Spender believe that it is necessary for creative endeavors to be preceded by conscious activities and work. To be able to create something one must work at assembling the necessary facts and analyzing the data that are available. You must define the problem and establish a goal in order to be able to search effectively for the solution. Then you must actively attempt to fit various solutions to the problem. Once you have done this, the subconscious mind has a better chance of creating the relevant solution to the problem. Let the facts float freely in the subconscious mind by engaging in periods of nondirective activities (sleep, walks, daydreaming).

Your clue to how good the resulting creative idea is may be called your "aesthetic susceptibilities." A solid creative idea somehow sounds good to you. Just as you are able to determine whether your actions are good or bad, you have this same kind of feeling about your creativity. Many times people make the mistake of expressing their new ideas to others who are openly skeptical of anything that is an innovation. Many good ideas are buried under unwarranted and unneeded attacks. It is better to hold off the presentation of something that is creative until you have had the opportunity to implement it and see the results. Creative thinking needs an enthusiastic reception.

Your aesthetic susceptibilities can be modified and improved through the application of principles of behavior modification. Behavioral psychologists believe that a person can control his own internal thought processes by symbolically producing consequences. Self-reinforcement of constructive thoughts is possible since you are aware of their occurrence and therefore can arrange for their contingencies.[2] Your appreciation of the worth and value of your thoughts can be controlled by your mental attitudes of good ideas and bad ideas. The self-control of your value system is arranged by engaging in activities that restrict the occurrence of negative cognitions.[3] If you do not allow yourself time to become overly critical of a creative idea, it will stand a much better chance of being maintained. Allow yourself many supporting activities of your ideas. Strengthen your ability to appreciate the value of your ideas by the self-reinforcement of positive lines of thought. Our self-generated mental values can determine the soundness of our creative ideas.

Personal value systems are the result of years of experiences, learning, personality structure, and several other factors. Values are the result of the process of socialization and being taught the difference between that which is a great idea and that which is no good at all. Idea appreciation—or as I have called it, aesthetic susceptibility—operates in terms of coverants in your mind. These symbolic operants follow the same principles of behavior modification as do your overt behaviors. And just as you can give yourself mental rewards (self-praise, self-confidence, and self-appreciation) for the successful accomplishment of your goals, the same type of rewarding system can be arranged for your creative abilities.

Creative Problem Solving

Creativity is the ability to find new solutions to problems that arise in one's environment. Seeking the challenge of new worlds is a good way of exposing yourself to new problems that demand unique solutions. Complex problems present us with an almost endless supply of seemingly relevant facts that might be used to solve the problem. Different people choose different problems to solve even in the same situations. Since there are numerous facts that can be picked from among many to find an answer, people come up with different solutions. This is an important reason not to talk to others about your creative solution to a problem. Another person may not see it in the same light that you have, and may reject your solution as being too ridiculous to work. The best way of determining the correctness of your solutions is through your own aesthetic susceptibilities and the results of the implementation. Many times academic training leads to what is called "analysis paralysis." This is a form of learned procrastination. Universities teach individuals how to go about sifting through the relevant facts for a problem solution, but there is no guidance in how problem solutions are to be implemented into the world.[4]

The steps in solving a problem are: (1) to define the problem, (2) to gather the relevant facts that will help arrive at a solution, (3) to decide on the possible courses of action that can be taken to solve the problem given the facts of the situation, (4) to evaluate the advantages and disadvantages of each alternative with your own system of internal aesthetic values, (5) to determine intuitively and subjectively the probability that the advantages and disadvantages will occur, (6) to pick the best alternative as you see it, (7) to carry out the decision by implementing it as quickly as possible, and (8) to evaluate the actual results against what you thought they would be.[5]

The Creative Process

The factors that are important in solving a problem also play a part in the development of creativity. There must be a mental orientation where you arrange yourself so that environmental problems are brought into focus. Firsthand experience is a method for problem orientation. When you travel, make notes about anything and everything that appeals to you. Become independent and try to rely on yourself to take care of your own personal needs. Becoming involved with people is one way of giving fuel to your creativity. Change from being passive to being an active doer of things. Try to do the things that you think you would like to try.

After you acquire a mental orientation, enter into periods of preparation where you gather the necessary facts for the possible solution to the problems that you have been exposed to. Creatively apply different facts in different combinations so that you can see unique solutions. Make analyses of the facts in relationship to the problems. Develop your own hypotheses about the various alternative ways of approaching the problem. Then let everything simmer through a period of nondirected activities. Do anything else that you want to do as long as you are not actively thinking about the problem solutions. Then suddenly without warning, the correct answer will surface in your conscious mind. You will feel that this is the solution that you have been searching for. Then do not make the mistake of procrastinating; put the answer into practice.

CREATIVE TECHNIQUES

There are hundreds of different things that people do in order to nurture and develop their creativity. The one thing that seems to offer the best method for pulling creative thoughts from a person is to arrange thinking contingencies. Structure your environment so that you are more likely to engage in creative thinking. Complete involvement and all-out intent to solve a problem remove distractions and help maintain periods of creativity. Sitting before a desk with paper and pencils on it can help you think. Removing alternative stimuli that compete for our attentions also help to increase our levels of concentration. And creativity requires concentrated efforts.

Practice and training are key elements in the development of your creativity. The Massachusetts Institute of Technology has opened its Innovation Center to train individuals in creative skills.[6] Everything from the conception of an idea to the implementation of inventions is taught at this special center at MIT.

Alex F. Osborn in his classic book on developing creativity—*Principles and Procedures of Creative Thinking*—gives several techniques for arranging for the occurrence of ideas.[7] He suggests that the setting of deadlines is helpful. Tension is a part of being creative. Many successful authors have learned to use tensions to develop their writing crafts from being journalists. Newspaper people learn to operate under deadlines, which are useful for an author to possess also. The most creative person sets for himself deadlines that require performance near the limits of his psychological endurance. The training that comes from working under pressure and deadlines improves the ability to be creative.

Creative skills are the result of training and practice. Practicing mental arithmetic for a few minutes a day for a week or two can result in the doubling of your ability to calculate mathematical problems. Your ability to form new images and to create new solutions to problems can be enhanced through practice. This is where the principles of behavior modification can be applied to help modify and maintain your creative abilities. Arrange the environment so that you are more likely to be rewarded for your ideas. Reinforce your ideas when you feel that they are good. Establish the proper contingencies for your creative behaviors. Rely on your own internal evaluations of when to self-reinforce the creative endeavor. Set aside particular times of the day for thinking about creative problem solutions. Put your ideas into action. Not only will this test their correctness, but also you will learn more about your ability to think by doing.

Techniques to Generate Ideas

The following techniques have been shown to lead to the emergence of various ideas. The basic idea behind almost all of the techniques is that the more ideas that one has, the better the chance is that a great one will be discovered. Apparently quantity leads to quality. All the possible techniques are not presented here. It is suggested that, if you are interested in learning about other techniques or more about the following ones, you consult any library.

Attribute listing involves selecting characteristics from one thing and applying them to something else in unique ways.[8] The use of checklists aids the discovery of new adaptations. Your ability to apply attributes from one situation to another depends to a large extent on the acuteness of your powers of observation.

Brainstorming has been a popular method for the generation of creative ideas.[9] With this method ideas are generated spontaneously from a group of people. The group is not allowed to criticize one another's ideas, but they strive for as many combinations of factors and new ideas as they can.

Another technique for arriving at new ideas is called morphological analysis.[10] The basic idea of this technique is to present the possible solutions to a problem in such a way as to lead one toward an evaluation of the solutions.[11]

Other techniques that can be found in any basic book on creativity are: running the alphabet, checklists, forcing relationships, synectics, and value analysis. Each of these techniques is noted for its ability to generate a quantity of new ideas.

Recently a technique has been used to advantage in developing individuals' powers of imagery and creativity. This technique uses the biofeedback machine that was discussed earlier. It has been found that artists are prolific producers of the brain rhythm known as alpha. These individuals get their images and ideas while they are in the theta state of brainwave activity. Researchers have reported that subjects trained to control their own alpha and theta states have been able to modify their hypnagogic states.[12] The hypnagogic state is filled with images and approaches the inner creative realm of the individual. Training in the control of one's brainwaves may lead to the ability to switch creativity on and off at will.

Conclusions

If you can improve your creative abilities, you will be a better writer, painter, poet, problem solver, and thinker. Creativity involves a period of preparation during which you must work diligently (at a conscious level) to gather the necessary facts and to apply them in alternative ways to solving a problem. This period of orientation to the situation may include the time you spend in becoming educated, observing, and experiencing life.

Creativity is improved whenever there is an environment conducive to that sort of behavior. The arrangement of one's environment is critically important to creative thought. Associate with others who are likely to positively reinforce your idea-generation. Stimulation by others is helpful in generating the proper atmosphere for creativity.

A period of nondirected activities is essential in order to let your subconscious mind search for the proper solution to the problem.

Creativity is like any other behavior. You know when you are creatively thinking and you can reward yourself for the proper responses. Creativity can be self-controlled.

13

Modifying your intellect

The self-improvement of your intellectual abilities is explored in this chapter. There are several methods that will increase your ability to speculate and think. Each of these methods can be self-controlled through the proper application of behavior modification principles. Active practices in learning, memory, studying, and reading can be maintained and controlled through environmental contingencies. Intellectual abilities can be improved and creativity strengthened with practice. The expression of your intellectual powers can be revealed through your creative writing skills. The principles of behavior modification will be structured to a writing program. The last part of this chapter shows you how you can effectively control your abilities to write.

The Creative Use of the Intellect

An intellectual person can be distinguished from other people by his ability to motivate himself to study and learn without someone prodding him to do it. A person who has a well-trained intellect is able to think logically and rationally. He has knowledge that he has acquired through the creative use of his intellect. An intellectual person is one who reads, learns, knows how to study efficiently, can think rationally, and has knowledge of things because of the development of his memory.

A challenging environment (at home, at work, and with others socially) definitely helps improve one's intelligence. Although the proper environment is critically important for babies, it is also important for the maintenance of an adult's mental skills and abilities. Arranging environmental contingencies for the performance of specific intellectual activities can effectively modify, maintain, and control your intellect and lead to an improvement in your intelligence. Mental self-stimulation can be used to develop your intellect.

Thinking effectively can be organized into three basic components. These components parallel the steps in complex problem solving and also of those involved in creative activities. Thinking starts with the task of acquiring a picture of the whole area that is to be dealt with. Then the most important elements are examined and analyzed as to their relationship to the total thing. Finally, these elements are somehow fitted back into the total area or problem. Creative thinking means that you are able to see the essential components of things and are then able to conceptually fit them back together.

To understand the workings of an automobile engine, you must be able to imagine the functions of the different parts. Once you have a clear idea of what each part does separately, you can conceptually see the workings of the whole engine. Thinking requires the ability to mentally discover the working parts of a task, and the creative ability to put them back together again in unique and hopefully better ways. Your success at this will be a function of the amount of practice that you do with your intellectual abilities.

Concentration

Concentration is necessary if you are to use the powers that you possess. Use the principle of establishing for yourself written goals and subgoals to force yourself to concentrate for a few minutes each day on specific subjects. The establishment of specific goals and the use of the personal contract with yourself will help to maintain your abilities to concentrate. In order to concentrate, you must establish attainable goals. Several experiments with the problem of concentration have shown that even with interesting areas of study, the attentions of people wander to other things in a short time. This may occur because people have failed to develop fully their powers of concentration. Establish a goal for yourself of two minutes of concentrated activity, which is followed by anything else that you like to do. Then concentrate again for two minutes. Keep repeating this schedule and gradually lengthen the time for concentration. Try to shoot for a goal of twenty minutes without having to pull your mind back to the required subject.

Thinking is a behavior that involves the use of various human capabilities and various acquired skills. The specific outcome of thinking behavior depends upon the environmental situation and the intellectual ability of the individual. Experience, problem-solving abilities, previous learning, and creativity are factors that tend to shape a person's thinking.

There are skills and drills that sharpen your thinking. Actions will enhance thinking. Write out your thoughts. Read books for answers to your questions. Talk to others and make notes on what they think. Practice logical thinking.

You cannot do any concentrated thinking when you are distracted. To improve your ability to engage in thinking behavior, arrange the stimulus situation so that the desired behavior will result. Find a quiet place that is free from competing stimuli. A bare room that is shut off from distractions is an ideal place for thinking.

Determine your goals for thinking. Decide on whether you are going to reinforce yourself for a certain number of ideas or for a particular length of time spent in thinking. Determine your rewards and punishments. Arrange the contingencies for the desired behaviors. The task of analyzing your personal thinking is to discover those situations in which you will respond by emitting thinking type behaviors. These behaviors must be brought under the control of the environment in which they occur.

Dewey's book *How We Think* (1911) suggests that as long

as the environment in which we place ourselves runs smoothly and consistently, our daily thinking will be done by habit. A routine life will be controlled by our emotions, gut reactions, and impulse. It is a stimulating environment filled with new challenges that causes us to think creatively with our intellects.

Learning

The principles of behavior modification rest on clinical and experimental evidence of the effects of experiences upon behavior. Behavior modification has been defined in terms of learning with the intent of improving an individual's ability to interact with his environment.[1] It is difficult for someone else to use operant conditioning on covert activities such as thinking because he is unable to observe the occurrence. But since you can determine when you are thinking, you can self-reward such behaviors even though they are not noticed by others. Whenever behaviors are properly rewarded (immediately after their occurrence, the proper schedule, and the right amount), these behaviors will tend to be repeated. Learning is rewarding in its own right, but for those who have not engaged in this activity for some time, it may be necessary to arrange for its contingencies until such time as learning can become self-rewarding.[2]

A potentially powerful technique for developing your learning capabilities has been demonstrated by Richardson in *Mental Imagery*.[3] Subjects were tested for their ability to throw darts and basketballs. Then instead of actually physically practicing these skills, the subjects were asked to imagine that they were performing these activities. They were to think about how they would improve their learning of the skills. At the end of two weeks of daily mental practice a significant improvement in the subjects' performance abilities was found. This improvement in learning came from thinking about the skills, and not from actual physical practice or any reinforcements.

Bugelski suggests that learning can come from merely thinking about something.[4] In some cases it is not necessary to take an active part in the learning process. The rewards for the ability to learn may be self-generated.

Memory

The well-developed intellect demands that you remember things. Intelligence is measured by the amount of knowledge that you command. Learning involves the use of previously acquired knowledge. You will waste much of your time if you forget most of what you have studied and read.

You must establish contingencies for memory behaviors. Without reinforcements, memory cannot be maintained or controlled. An important aspect of remembering things is motivation. If there is no reason to remember a phone number because you will never call it, then your motivation for committing it to your memory is close to nil. The first step in remembering things is to want to remember them. Develop an interest in learning to remember.

Arrange your environment so that distractions will be minimized. Make use of your powers of observation. Concentrate upon the learning task.

There are several well-known procedures to develop memory. The most widely used one is repetition. Memory is the conditioned association between things. The more times these things are repeated the better they will be remembered.

Other techniques to help your memory are grouping, numerical method, alphabet arrangement, topical systems, peg systems, and link systems. Some excellent memory books are given in the chapter references in this book. You should be able to apply this book's techniques for self-control to those memory methods.

After you have discovered a memory technique that you think will aid you in remembering things, apply the principles of behavior modification to its use. Arrange your environmental contingencies so that you can concentrate on using the technique. Reward those behaviors that lead to better memory. Develop your powers of concentration by restricting competing stimuli. Decide on a goal that you want to attain. As an example, this goal may be to spend twenty minutes every day on practicing the memory techniques. Design a behavioral schedule and write out your personal contract to stay with it until you have attained the goal that you are seeking. Start by giving yourself rewards for remembering things. Soon the ability to remember will in itself become self-reinforcing.

How to Control Your Studying

No one can force you to sit down at a desk and study. But the principles of behavioral control are available if you desire to increase the amount of time you spend in study behaviors. Some common excuses for not studying are: (1) tried to study several times but never been able to do it; (2) always think of other things more fun to be doing than studying; (3) too many distractions and noises to concentrate; and, (4) do not feel like studying.

You may consciously want to study. You gather the necessary materials to aid you in this task. But when you place yourself in the study position, you are not quite able to behave in the proper manner that is necessary to learn the material. You may procrastinate and put off your study behavior. As a deadline gets nearer, you begin to get panicky and unable to concentrate. You may daydream while at the desk.

To control your study behavior you must make a self-determination of the conditions that are causing your study behaviors *and* your nonstudy behaviors. If the environment is too noisy for you to concentrate on studying, then you must arrange for an environment that is more conducive to your studying behaviors. Arrange and apply the various principles of behavior modification to your study activities just as you would to any other behavior. Study can be self-controlled.

A person who can study efficiently is one who schedules specific times for that activity. And he does only study activities in those specific times. These people know how to use various information sources. And most importantly, they know how to structure their environment so that the stimuli that compete for their study behaviors are restricted, and the proper reinforcing environmental contingencies follow the performance of the desired study behaviors.

The following list contains principles that you can use to

control your study behaviors.[5] Each of these principles or techniques can be self-controlled and will result in effective study behaviors.

1. Pick a certain time that you will begin studying each day. Do not randomly study different subjects at different times of the day.

2. Be consistent in your studying. Do not let your time for studying a particular subject go by without spending the self-determined amount of time in studying it.

3. Determine the number of minutes that you will spend in studying a certain subject. Start with a small number. Remember it is much better to spend ten minutes a day every day studying a subject than it is to spend an hour daydreaming about a trip to Europe, especially if your goal is to study more.

4. When the time you have scheduled for study is over, get up and leave the area. Also, if you find your mind wandering to other subjects while you are supposed to be studying, get up and go somewhere else until you can devote your entire attention to the subject.

5. Decide upon some form of aversive reinforcement for your failure to meet the terms of your agreement.

6. Decide upon what to reward yourself with, and when to do so, after you have accomplished a certain amount of study.

7. Put these into your personal contract with yourself.

8. Stick to your agreement.

Try to keep the aversive conditions of this self-imposed study schedule small by not forcing yourself to stay at a study position for long periods of time.

The preceding are the behavioral principles that will help you spend gradually longer periods of time in the study of various things. These are procedures that will put you into study positions. These principles will help you maintain your desire to study. They will not replace the factors that are necessary to learn the material. The use of techniques like the following will increase your ability to learn: making a written summary of things that you have just finished reading; consciously attempting to recall what you have studied; describing learned material to others trying to practice what you are studying; putting the material into different contexts; and, developing a desire to learn as much as you can about a subject.

The idea of scheduling a ten-minute-a-day study period followed by a reward may seem too simple to be an effective method of controlling a complex intellectual activity like studying. But, in numerous experimental studies and self-control practices, simple techniques have led to permanent changes in complex behavioral activities.

Self-Education

The most efficient method for acquiring an education is by reading. It is not easy to acquire knowledge on one's own without someone to motivate you. Achievement without effort is impossible. Reading with understanding and thinking logically is not easy. Universities seem to be slipping toward letting students get degrees without having to put any effort into things that they do not feel like doing. A university education does not mean that an individual is educated intellectually. You can arrange the contingencies for your own educational program. Active inquiry and a well-rounded reading program are necessary to acquire the knowledge for becoming an educated person.

To truly educate yourself, you must develop the habit of thinking and learning as you read selectively. Reading, if done with an inquiring mind and positive attitude, is the best way to educate yourself.

Based upon the principles of operant conditioning, a new form of teaching book has been successful in many self-education programs. These books are called "programmed learning" texts or books. They operate on the principles of gradual learning steps and immediate reinforcements. These books present a piece of information, then ask a question to see if you understand it completely. There is a series of questions followed by answers. By sliding a card down the page, you can answer a question and immediately see whether or not your answer is correct. Knowledge of the results, even though your answer may have been incorrect, is reinforcing. As you read and study your way through a programmed learning text, you are constantly reinforced for your learning. There are something like 5,000 titles of programmed learning books. Some of the things that you can educate yourself about with these programmed texts are: how to write, using a slide rule, chemistry, calculus, marketing, sailing, and how to create a programmed textbook.

Increasing Reading and Comprehension

Reading fast without remembering what you have read is a waste of your time. The real purpose of reading is to get information (how to make a million in the stock market) or for pleasure (the mystery thriller of the century). It is not necessary to see each and every word. A fast reader, who is able to comprehend much of what he has read, skims over the material skipping much. Trying to find typographical errors is not the way to read for understanding. Slow readers talk to themselves. Their lips move, and you can feel the subvocalizations if you put your hand on their throats.

You can train yourself to read at faster and faster rates. Speed and concentration can be developed at the same time. As with your other self-control tasks, you should set a goal for your reading. Understanding of the material should not be your first consideration in the establishment of objectives for reading. The ability to remember the passages that you have read will result if you concentrate on the things that you are reading, no matter how fast you are reading.

As a first step in increasing your reading speed, make a determination of your present reading speed. Select a chapter in this book or another and read consistently for several minutes. Find out the number of words that you have read by finding the number of words per line of type. Multiply this by the number of lines per page, and then multiply this by the actual number of pages that you read. Dividing this number of words by the number of minutes it took you to read them will give you the words per minute that you can read. This average is your base line for your present reading abilities.

Set your goal to double your base line rate. A normal person reads about 200 words per minute. To double your reading rate you must push yourself to read larger and larger numbers of words. Each day schedule yourself twenty to thirty minutes for improving your reading speed. Gradually increase your reading speed by attempting to read more words per unit of time. Select longer passages and try to read them in a fixed unit of time. Buy yourself a book just to practice increasing your speed.

Keep a daily chart of the changes in your reading speed. Each day set a timer and read quickly for five minutes. Rest and read again for five minutes. Summarize the material you have been reading. Practice remembering the material you read, even though you may be missing some as you force your speed up. Within two or three weeks of consistent practice your reading speed will be at least twice what you started with.

Comprehension may fall a little at first as you push your reading speed, but many individuals report increases in their ability to recall passages that they have read. Increases in comprehension at rapid reading speeds can be attributed to an increase in concentration. At 500 or more words per minute, a person just does not have time to think about anything but his reading.

There will be a tendency to fall back to your more comfortable base-line rate if you do not keep self-control. Establish contingencies for your reading so that the behaviors that you have improved upon will not deteriorate.

Writing Self-Control

You can use the principles from behavior modification to better organize, control, and improve your writing abilities.

A writer is one who writes. This will be the starting point for the application of the behavioral control principles. Style will not be taught. Nor will grammar, spelling, how to plot a story, developing characters, or where to sell a book. These are non-writing activities. Behavioral principles will be applied to the problem of your getting as many words onto the piece of paper as you can.

Many aspiring writers spend much of their lives learning

what they suppose are the crafts of the writing trade. Some believe that an education will open the writing door to them. There are many Ph.D.'s who are unable to make themselves understood in their writings. A professor recently submitted an article for possible publication in a scholarly and prestigious journal that was read by some of the smartest people in the world. The professor's article was rejected on the grounds that it was too esoteric—his writing style was too verbose to be understood by the editors of the journal. This is a classic example of an individual who spent many years in becoming an expert in his field, who possessed great intellectual gifts, and had complete knowledge of a particular subject, but was unable to be understood by his own intellectual equals.

You do not have to have a doctorate degree in English in order to be a writer. It has often been said that everyone has the experiences for at least one story.

People who want to write but never get around to actually putting words on the paper are unable to practice self-control. Procrastination in the form of doing research is a common method of stalling the writing of an article or book. Skilled writers can spend an hour or so in researching a topic and then are able to write about it for hours. Reporters spend a little time in observing an event; the majority of their time is spent writing about what they saw. Hopeful writers maintain that they must acquire a broad and complete understanding of the subject that they are going to write about. Several books that have been well-received have been written by people who knew little about a particular subject. An expert in a field probably would be unable to write well about that area since he would not have the necessary time to spend in writing.

Your writing goal should be to get a certain number of words on paper. During the writing of the first draft do not worry about the style, grammar, or other things as much as you do about getting as many words as you can on paper in a certain amount of time. You should not worry about style or reaching any particular market. Set for yourself a goal of some number of words. The average book today contains roughly 100,000 words. Some authors have finished a 200,000-word manuscript in as little as three months. You can do the same.

Using a pencil as the writing instrument (you can write many more words per minute with a typewriter), you can write a stream of words that average twenty-five per minute, or about 1,500 per hour. Working eight hours per day for nine days will net you 108,000 words. An average typist can type twice as fast as you can write with the pencil. If you could develop the methods of self-control, you could write the necessary number of words for a book in two weeks. Of course, a book is more than just a series of words strung together. But we shall only look at the arrangement of environmental contingencies to control word count not literary style. Writing a certain number of words is an easier behavior to control than some of the other elements that go into a piece of writing because you can objectively measure (count) the number of words.

Writing behavior can be controlled with the same contingencies that maintain a pigeon's pecking responses. Operant conditioners have trained animals on schedules of reinforcement that required thousands of responses. The same principles apply to your writing behavior. Set subgoals. After every twenty minutes of writing, stop and do something else that is rewarding. Then go back to the writing. Writing for two hours a day, every day, is a goal of many established authors.

A goal of a certain amount of time spent in writing means that other activities are not engaged in. Writing is the physical act of putting words upon paper. If you spend part of your two hours daydreaming and researching, you have not written for two hours. If necessary, establish other hours in the day for activities that are tangent to writing and that will help supplement your craft. But if you contract with yourself to write a specified number of hours each day, then make sure that you stick by it.

Writing is lonely, hard work. It is an activity that may not be rewarding in itself. To develop your control of your writing behaviors it will be necessary to establish reinforcing contingencies to maintain and strengthen that behavior. This is easily done by determining a reward and giving it to yourself whenever your behaviors reach your self-determined subgoals. Write into the contract that you develop at the start of the writing program those contingencies that will help you accomplish your goals. For example, after the completion of each ten pages of writing, you get to have a cold drink of water and a five-minute nap.

Obtain a timer and set it for thirty-minute intervals. Work steadily and consistently while under the stimulus control of the timer. When it rings, stop your writing. I have found it rewarding to do one minute of exercises after each thirty minutes of writing. Once you have determined a schedule, do not get sidetracked into other activities. If you have designed a writing program that specifies two hours a day at a certain time that will be spent writing, do not change your program to watch a special on the television. Check the listings at the start of the week and schedule television watching into your control program so that you still write for two hours each day.

Writing for periods longer than two hours a day requires the scheduling of different activities so that you do not suffer from boredom and discomfort from doing too much of one thing. The following is a schedule that might be adapted to your needs:

15 minutes—organization of writing materials;
1 hour—writing (no research, no daydreaming, no reading);
30 minutes—reading;
30 minutes—additional research for the next period of writing;
2 minutes—following a self-designed program of exercises;
1 hour—writing;

and I start over on the reading, researching and exercising portions of the schedule. I write four hours a day with this technique. I regularly give myself reinforcements.

Only about one in a thousand people who want to write a book ever start. Only about one percent of those ever finish what they have started. The reason usually is that it takes too long to finish a book. Facing a task that involves writing 100,000 words seems impossible. If you are going to write, you must do two things. First, you must make the start. Procrastination will not finish the book for you. Second, you must divide the task into manageable and attainable units. Work toward a goal of an hour a day and you will be able to write a book in three or four months. Think of it. A book in three months by writing only an hour a day. Writing is an easy behavior to self-control.

14

The self-control of your success

To many, success is defined in terms of their accumulation of money. For other people, success may be a finished book or painting, good friends, a life filled with experiences, or happiness. There may be as many examples of success as there are people striving for their goals. Success is your inner satisfactions, not those of society.

Success starts with an analysis of yourself. The program for the attainment of personal success must grow out of your likes and then build upon them as a framework. The essentials necessary for success are: a positive attitude, motivation, and desire. Your ability to reach your goal of success depends upon your ability to exploit environmental opportunities. And you must have discipline to stick to a plan for achieving personal success.

There have been many studies of successful people and of people who have failed. One study of 25,000 people who felt that they failed revealed that the major cause was a lack of decision. The people procrastinated long enough that opportunity for success would vanish. Successful people decide upon a course of action and act upon it.

There are many approaches to obtaining success and the approach taken in this chapter is based upon the principles of behavior modification. The type of success attainment that will be discussed in this chapter will be business or monetary. But regardless of the kind of success that you are seeking, you can break the attainment of the goal into the following broad factors:

    1. A specific and obtainable goal.

    2. The development of a concrete, specific plan for the attainment of the goal.

    3. Initiation of the behaviors that will result in the goal being reached.

What They Pictured in Their Minds Came True

I do not believe in telling people that if they only use their willpower they will become successful. Wishing that you were successful does not make you a success. An alternative approach to success maintains that if you only work hard enough you will become successful. Only by actually performing the necessary behaviors will one acquire the trappings of success. You must decide upon what you want and engage in those activities that will bring you and the desired goal together. A person who continually dreams of how he will spend the great wealth that he believes in will not accomplish anything but the title "a lazy dreamer."

Thinking about growing rich is only a flight of your imagination unless you couple this attitude with direct actions and behaviors that will let you reach your goal for success. The viable alternative to dreaming about success is the establishment of a self-control program that will provide for environmental contingencies for the behaviors that lead to your idea of personal success. The principles of behavior modification can be applied to your behavior so that you will achieve the goal of success.

Success involves the following factors: a period of active work; efforts and energies that are expended to bring you into a stream leading toward the goal. You must possess understanding of the factors that you will use in becoming successful. If you intend to be successful with a business of your own, you must know about accounting, finance, marketing, the products that you will sell, and so on. You must take an idea, develop an action plan for it, and so structure the business functions that the proper combination of ingredients will result in your successful new business venture.

Even though you may realize what it takes to become successful, you may not know how to get started. Years of wishful thinking may have blunted your willpower or resolve to undertake some long and complex activity. You lack the proper motivation to start working toward a far-off goal like success.

There are several firms that claim to be able to teach you the secret to "Success" or "Quick Riches." The secret supposedly lies in these firms' abilities to motivate you toward success. These firms charge up to $500 for their secrets. They offer no real guarantees for your chances of success and the attainment of great personal fortunes. Before you spend several hundred dollars for motivation via a recorded message, ask yourself why you could not motivate yourself. Each success school or motivational firm was started by an individual (or a small group). Not one motivational-success firm has ever claimed to have become successful from their enrollment in a program that taught success! Can you buy motivation? I do not know, but there are definite keys that will help you develop motivation for some task—and these keys are within you and are modifiable through self-control.

The Principles of Success

You possess the factors necessary for success. Your desire for personal satisfaction must be mixed with your talents and abilities. Talents, skills, and abilities can be learned when you have the desire. The attainment of success will result from your development of a personal program of self-control that utilizes specific goals and behaviors.

The plan that you develop for obtaining the goal is important if you are to know where you are headed and how you will get there.

1. Establish a measurable goal. This can take the form of answers to questions like: What sales do I want to reach? How much net profit do I desire at the end of the next six months? What do I want my net worth to be in one year or two?

2. What behaviors will be necessary to obtain my goals?

Each action that you engage in must be related to the successful attainment of the desired end. No one knows what the result of his actions will be before he implements them, so it is vital that you assess your actions throughout your success program. If you are doing something that is hurting the attainment of your goal, develop alternative responses along the way.

3. Maintain records of the actions and their results as you implement your decisions.

4. Be flexible in your approach to success. Change your program if it appears to be leading you in the wrong direction.

Success Goals

You must define your purposes. If you are attempting to acquire money, state in writing exactly how much you will earn by a certain date. It is not enough to tell yourself—"I want a lot of money." Instead say—"I will earn $100,000 in the next two years." Anywhere from 80 to 90 percent of those wanting to be successful never are because they do not have a definite purpose. Write down your goal, and you will understand better how to act in order to reach it. It may be helpful to spend an hour or two in structuring your goal of success in your mind and then writing down the final version.

Contractual Deadline

Develop a specific plan for the attainment of the goal. Set a deadline that can be met and enter into a contractual agreement with yourself to work toward that goal with the plan that you have developed. Establish a daily schedule for recording and reviewing your performances. Attempt to develop internal self-reinforcements for behaviors that lead you to the attainment of the goal. Successful people are able to determine whether or not they are behaving in the manner necessary for the attainment of their success.

Procrastination

Start working on your success now. Use whatever skills you now have and find better ones as you work your way to the goal.

Procrastination can cost you a potential fortune. If you wanted to, you could gather facts for months to help in the solution of a complex business problem. Marketers are interested in learning the effectiveness of their advertisements. They would like to know the answer to questions like: Which of these commercials will convince more people to buy our product?

Business people must be careful about spending too much time in analyzing the situations in which they must operate and sell their products. A firm hired a market research group to determine which of two product designs would be better received by consumers. The researchers established test market situations with the two products and were able to find out consumers' attitudes toward the products. The data were turned over to a statistician to see which product design was better. The results of the study were subjected to intensive statistical analysis. The variables were correlated, a polynomial regression was run, the data were transformed into another form so that a multiple step regression coefficient could be applied, and finally a canonical correlation was used to determine if there was an awareness of product differences that could be attributed to the functions of the variables. It took considerable time and money to perform these calculations and analyses. The final conclusion was that it did not matter which one of the designs was used. Consumers would accept them equally. But the problem was that by the time the analyses were completed, the market situation had changed and a competitor had already introduced a similar product. The firm lost its competitive advantage through a process of statistical procrastination. The analysis had paralyzed the implementation process.

SALESMANSHIP

Sales are an excellent way to earn an above average income. In most sales jobs, you are paid in direct relationship to the amount of sales that you make. This means that the harder you work the more sales that you will make, and the more money that you will earn. But sales positions also present something of a problem. Unless you can practice self-control, you may not be able to make as many sales as you should. It takes will power to call on customers when you are an independent salesperson.

If you want to improve your selling abilities, you can use the principles of behavior modification to help you. But these principles will work only if you use them. Self-control will literally open a new world of personal accomplishment in becoming an improved salesperson.

Procrastination is the ruin of many salespeople. They can spend an entire afternoon looking at luxury cars and daydreaming about the day that they would buy one or two of those fancy cars. If only they would spend more time selling to make more money, rather than dreaming about it! It is easy to deviate from selling behaviors. Each day salespeople begin with good intentions to make many sales that day, and end that day with a bitter feeling toward themselves because of the wasted time they let themselves engage in. You can control this kind of waste by developing a schedule, entering into an agreement with yourself, and abiding by your personal contract.

A self-control program for sales will benefit from the daily recording and graphing of sales contacts. Buy yourself an inexpensive plastic counter to keep track of the number of sales attempts that you make each day. Keep track of your phone calls, the number of business cards that you leave with people, and the number of clients that you talk to. Get some charting paper and graph each day's selling behavior. The daily charts will be your record, which you can check against your initial base line and your personal agreement with yourself. These daily charting activities will protect your self-control program from irregular and half-hearted selling attempts.

One of the best things about the principles of behavior modification is that you can use them to control your own individual behaviors. Everything is self-contained. The controls on your selling behaviors are self-maintained and self-regulated. You can design a sales improvement program that will fit your style of selling.

Decide upon a sales goal. Be specific. If you decide that your goal is to be more sales, then tell yourself—"Within the next three weeks I will call upon fifty new customers." Be reasonable and do not expect to stay with a self-improvement program that requires calling upon everyone in the telephone book in the next week. State your goal in the form of a written agreement.

Reward your selling behaviors. If you reach what you consider is a good level of sales today, go to that movie tonight. If you failed to live up to your self-imposed set of standards, deny yourself your favorite television program. To improve upon the number of sales calls that you make, arrange for immediate reinforcements whenever you finish a sales presentation.

The value of a salesperson is measured by a factor that is almost nonexistent among others who regularly receive paychecks. As an independent seller, you have to be the master of yourself. Self-control principles will help to turn your wasted time into productive and successful hours.

15

Controlling your bad habits

You probably do several things that you wish you did not do. Excessive eating, drinking, smoking, nail-biting, or other unwanted habits are behaviors that can be self-controlled. But trying to cure a phobia will be easier than breaking your bad habits. Habits have their rewards already built in. You have to work hard to self-control a habit.

There are difficulties with attempting to self-control your bad habits. They are immediately rewarding. Eating a piece of pie feels better than trying to ignore a feeling of hunger. The negative effects of alcohol do not show up until the next morning; while you are drinking, you feel good. A second difficulty with attempting to self-control your habits is the doubts you have about your abilities to control your desires with a few simple instructions and techniques. Generally, the most effective method of altering habitual behaviors has been with the aid of someone else. Habits can be replaced with alternative behaviors that are more constructive, but it requires a consistent self-control program to maintain the new behaviors.

If you want to control any of your behaviors, you must establish the environment that will control those behaviors. You can get rid of the sight of food. You can sell the television set.

You can throw away all the cigarettes. You can pour out all the alcohol that may be around the house. This chapter looks at the self-control of two habits that are difficult to break—overeating and smoking. To help you in your resolve to control these behaviors you must do two things. One, you must arrange the environmental contingencies so that the behaviors will be modified. Two, you must follow closely the principles of behavior modification so that you can effectively keep your self-control.

Eating Less and Enjoying It More

The problem with trying to control overeating is that you need food. But food is a stimulus that causes you to think about eating. As long as you do not have to think about food, you do not have a desire to eat. If you did not eat so much, you would not be overweight.

It is not any trouble to lose weight. Many people have lost weight by eating diet foods, going to exercise salons, taking drugs, being psychoanalyzed, and by being shocked each time they ate. There is absolutely no problem in getting rid of a couple pounds. A crash diet will let you lose ten pounds in a week or two. There is no problem in locating some fad diet to help you to lose a few pounds. There are water diets, noncarbohydrate diets, macrobiotic diets, and protein-only diets. Many of these diets are unhealthy for you in two ways. You may lose the weight too quickly. A drastic change in body weight upsets the physiological processes. Also, chemical imbalances result from eating too much of one kind of food and not enough of others.

To attempt to lose more than a few pounds of body weight is a serious undertaking. Find out about how much you should weigh by referring to charts that take into consideration height, body type, and age. Develop a time schedule for your weight reduction program. Decide upon the food that you will and will not eat. Decide upon an excercise program to supplement your food control plan. Follow the self-control principles that have been suggested in this book—set your goals, arrange the contingencies, sign the personal contract with yourself, make certain that the desired behavioral changes are kept small. When all these activities have been completed, go see a doctor for a physical examination. He will be better able to determine if your program for losing weight will be safe for you.

To lose weight you must reduce the number of calories that you take in and/or increase the number of calories that you use. Whenever we attempt to reduce caloric intake, we get a feeling of hunger. Hunger is not a rewarding experience and your tendency is to quit the nonrewarding diet. Anytime you enter into a program to lose weght that requires a painful hunger feeling, you are drastically reducing the chances for staying on that program. You must make the self-control program for your weight loss as pleasurable as you can. You can do this by bringing about a gradual reduction in weight and by arranging for pleasurable alternative activities to take your mind off food.

A simple technique to help you reduce the amount of food you eat is to force yourself to eat slowly. It is not the quantity of food that fills us up. No matter how much food you try to force down, a feeling of being full does not result until twenty minutes have passed. Set up your self-control program so that you have to spend twenty minutes eating the same amount of food that you normally eat. Try chewing each piece of food ten or fifteen times. Lay your fork down between bites. Do not hurry your meal. I have found that I eat less but still feel full if I drink a glass of water about five or ten minutes before the meal. Substituting a glass of water for a candy bar is a good way of controlling hunger feelings while at the same time not taking in additional calories.

A program of exercises should be established to complement your weight-reduction program. Physical exercises are not effective by themselves in helping a person lose weight. The proper diet must be followed even though you regularly work out. You have to walk for an hour, swim for an hour, and run for half an hour just to burn off the calories from one hamburger and a malted milk!

A program of exercises should be kept to manageable amounts. Designing a schedule for yourself involving running three miles, 100 push-ups, and doing two hours of assorted sports will lead to such discomfort that you will quickly drop out of your self-improvement program.

You should use some method for determining your daily weight loss. A set of bathroom scales is helpful. Weigh yourself each day and keep a record of it to compare against your base line or starting weight. Deviations from the base line will be reinforcing to you. Scales and graphs are good, but the success of your weight-loss program will depend upon your self-control.

There are some tricks to help you in your self-improvement program. Wear tight clothes to your meals. They act as stimuli to remind you that you are eating too much. Drink less caffeinated beverages. Caffeine lowers the blood sugar level of the body, and you feel hungry. Drink lots of water, especially just before a meal. Eat only at certain times of the day. This means that you must stop eating snacks during the day whenever you start to feel hungry. And remember less than 5 percent of all the people who diet are able to modify their behaviors so that they do not gain the weight back. Therefore, you must learn to control your eating through the applications of the principles for self-control and continue to practice the techniques so that you will keep those pounds of fat from coming back.

Aversive Consequences

In the long run, excessive weight can cause heart problems. Being fat does not feel good, nor does an extremely overweight person look good. These are some of the aversive consequences that result from a lack of control of eating behaviors. If being fat results in these negative consequences, why do people continue to eat as they do? Because eating is immediately rewarding.

Clinical psychologists have been attempting to reduce the immediate gratification that comes from eating. They do this to help fat people reduce the amount of food that they are eating. Punishments have been used with some success in controlling appetites. Electric shockers have been attached to patients' forks to discourage excessive and rapid eating. If insufficient time elapses between the lifting of the fork, the patients receive a shock. The researchers are not attempting to stop the eating behavior, only to slow it down. Sometimes they shock the patients for eating the wrong kinds of food—candy, ice cream, and so forth. Some patients have lost almost 100 pounds with this procedure. As yet the technique has been used only in a hospital under the supervision of a physician.

The method of covert desensitization has been used to control excessive eating behaviors. The patient imagines eating something really good. The substance is described in great detail, and when the subject begins to chew upon it it begins to taste like excrement. The patient is supposed to generalize the imagined taste to excess food that they want to eat. The method reduces one's desire for food. This procedure can be changed slightly and used to advantage to help you reduce your desires for food. Try eating as much fat as you can. Eat it until you actually get nauseated from the thought of fat. Whenever you get the urge to eat more than you should, remember the gobs of fat that you ate.

A Self-Control Program for Weight Control

Mary Harris developed a weight control program that resulted in permanent loss of weight for several of the patients who took part in the experiment.[1] The program used no aversive consequences, nor did it cause any changes in the subjects' moods. The program was established so that the individuals that took part in it were in control of their own weight loss. Harris did not use any threats, punishments, drugs, or rigid diet rules in the program. The individuals' eating patterns were established by the people themselves; therefore they were more likely to follow their own guidelines.

Harris used three techniques to alter eating behaviors. First, the people were told about the immediate reinforcing effects of their eating activities. It was explained to them that their behaviors were under the stimulus control of food, and that the negative effects of eating too much were delayed.

To help you to see the consequences of your eating behaviors, make a list of the positive and negative reasons for being fat. My list looks like the following:

1. Being fat provides some insulation against the elements.
2. Being fat means that the heart has to pump blood through extra miles of capillaries.
3. Fat people are known to be happier.
4. A fat person looks bad.
5. Food tastes good, therefore a lot of food is good.
6. People who are not fat live longer.

The second technique that Harris used was to limit the situations in which eating could take place. Give food the respect that it demands. Eat as much as you desire, but do not eat while engaged in such activities as studying, watching television, or reading. Stop eating between meals and at places other than at the table.

The third technique that Harris used to control eating behaviors was to get the people to eat more slowly.

Harris did not use punishments to control the eating behaviors, but she did use aversive counterconditioning to control the desires for food. The complete control of these aversive consequences was left with the individuals. They were merely taught the technique of thinking about certain nauseating situations whenever they felt a craving for a particular food.

It was emphasized throughout the training program that the techniques were only suggestions on how to alter eating behaviors and that the techniques would work differently for each person. The best method for the control of eating was through the proper application of self-controls.

You must experiment to find the right mixture of techniques to best control yourself. The principles of behavior modification will allow you to tailor a diet program to your individual needs and requirements. The following is an outline of the principles that can be used to self-control your eating habits.

1. Determine how much you want to weigh.
2. Record your present weight and enter it as a base line upon a graph.
3. Develop and sign a personal agreement with yourself to follow a particular course of action to reach your goal.

4. Establish the contingencies to maintain your behaviors.
5. Weigh yourself daily and record the results.
6. Determine the aversive consequences for failure to stay with your diet program.
7. Determine the rewards that you shall give to yourself.
8. Follow the techniques to help you lose weight. These are: keep food hidden, drink a glass of water before eating, wear tight clothes, etc.
9. Eat only at specific times and at certain places.
10. Develop a program of exercises.
11. Use covert desensitization.
12. Develop competing behaviors that will take the place of eating behaviors. Take a walk instead of eating lunch.

Self-Control of Smoking

The breaking of the habit of smoking will not be the easiest behavior to change, but it can be controlled. If you can determine the reinforcers that are maintaining your smoking habit, you can set up the environmental contingencies that will counteract their effectiveness. For example, if you find that you smoke because it helps to keep weight down by curbing your appetite, you can develop a program of exercises that will help you lose any unnecessary weight and condition an incompatible response. But regardless of the reason why you smoke, the only proven way to stop smoking is to develop and practice self-control.

Smoking is a way of manipulating the environment. This control of the environment is reinforcing. The smoke exhaled, ashes that form on the end of the cigarette, handling the light or matches, the change in the cigarette's length, and the taste of the tobacco are reinforcing to the smoker.

Smoking may be controlled through the use of aversive contingencies. You can make yourself sick by smoking all the cigarettes possible in a short time. Each time that you think about the experience, you will experience mental discomfort and maybe some nausea. The purpose of satiating yourself with smoking is to reduce the imagined pleasure that you get from smoking. Punishments may be used to stop your smoking behavior. Being shocked each time that you light up a cigarette is effective in controlling smoking behavior. But this method works only as long as the punishment is being used.

You can gradually put more and more obstacles in the path of your smoking, so that at some point it just is not worth all the trouble and you will stop smoking. Writing down when, where, what time, and why you smoke each cigarette helps to reduce the desire for the smoke.

Restricting the times and places where you can smoke will help you to stop. Only smoking where there are no other activities occurring will tend to make smoking less fun. Restricting yourself to the basement for smoking takes some of the pleasure out of the habit.

The establishment of a competing response to take the place of smoking is an effective approach. This alternative response must be reinforcing in itself, or you will not stick with it. Chewing on gum is used by many to help make the transition.

Rewarding nonsmoking behavior is useful in reducing smoking.

Make a public pledge that you are not going to smoke. This approach, like the use of punishment, will work only if it is used in conjunction with some other self-control principle. Telling people that you are quitting a bad habit is only as effective in stopping your behavior as is the power of your self-control.

Develop a strong program for self-control based upon the principles presented in this book:

Establish a goal—are you going to stop completely by such a date, or are you just going to reduce the number of cigarettes that you smoke per day?

Write the goal down and sign an agreement with yourself to work toward that goal.

Count and graph daily the cigarettes that you smoke.

Reward those days in which you are able to meet or beat your subgoals. Use some form of aversive consequences whenever your behaviors do not reach the level established in your personal contract.

Reduce the temptations for smoking by arranging the environment so that you will not fall under the stimulus control of cigarettes. The sight of a package of cigarettes is sufficient to cause you to desire one. You are less likely to be reminded of smoking when there are not any triggering cues present. Get rid of all the cigarettes that may be seen.

Develop a list of positive and negative factors that smoking a cigarette brings to your mind. Each time you think about smoking and each time you light a cigarette think about the list. Look back at page 54 of this book to see a suggested list of positive and negative statements that can be used to reduce your smoking behavior.

16

A better life through self-control

You can control yourself. The ability to arrange your life so that you will become what you want to be can be achieved without years of costly psychotherapeutic guidance. The principles and techniques for bringing about desired behavioral changes in yourself can be applied without assistance. You control yourself. This book has presented the principles, facts, framework, and conclusions for a self-improvement program that you can use to control any of your behaviors. Since you are aware of your internal psychological states, you can do something that another person cannot do. You can modify your intellectual abilities with the principles of behavior modification. You can self-control and self-improve any of your behaviors. Practicing the techniques of self-control will help you to live a better life.

If after reading this book you are still unable to achieve self-control, one of the following conditions may be responsible:

1. The goal that you established was too difficult to reach. You expected the impossible from yourself.

2. The goal was too vague. Do not say that you will think yourself rich. Be specific.

3. There were no immediate consequences for the performances.

4. The behaviors that you engaged in did not lead to the accomplishment of the goal.

5. You did not have enough desire to maintain your self-control program.

6. You were not consistent in working toward the goal.

7. You did not record the daily occurrences of the behaviors.

8. You lied to yourself by failing to abide by the personal contract that you signed.

It is your fault if you fail to achieve self-control. The general principles and techniques have been developed from clinical situations in which their effectiveness has been proven with patients who had severe psychological problems. The principles of behavior modification are stronger in some instances than drugs or electroshock therapy. If you truly want to change your behaviors, you can do it through the application of self-control techniques. Once you have used self-control to modify your behavior and have seen how effective it is, you will enjoy the feeling of power that you have over yourself.

Basic Principles for Your Self-Improvement

Giving yourself reinforcements will modify your behaviors.

Select a rewarding activity and make it contingent upon the performance of some desired behavior, and you will gain control of that behavior.

Positive consequences lead to permanent changes in your behaviors, and negative consequences lead to temporary changes in your behaviors.

Knowing that you can control yourself is rewarding.

Self-reinforcing activities and rewards are necessary to maintain self-control until the benefits of changing the behavior take over that function.

A personal, written contract will reduce your deviations from the self-improvement program.

Goals must be specific, reasonable, and obtainable.

Your deviations from your contract will be met with negative self-evaluations, and these will help you to stay with your program.

Changes in behaviors must be kept gradual.

Use objective records of your performances.

Learning relaxation will help you to develop self-control.

Images and thoughts of both positive and negative things can reinforce your behaviors.

Daily commitments to your self-control program are highly recommended.

Any behavior can be controlled.

The Program

This is a program for your self-control that will help you improve yourself. This program will turn your wasted hours into golden hours of self-improvement. It may not be an easy task to change something that you have been doing for years, but it will not be an impossible task if you keep the desired changes gradual and offer yourself rewards for successful accomplishments.

All that you have to do is follow a few simple instructions and self-control skills will become second nature to you.

You can develop whatever you want for yourself starting *right now*.

Self-control can be accomplished by _____.

Self-improvement is controlled entirely by _____.

A self-improvement program does what you want it to for _____.

The answer to all the above blanks is
YOU

Your personal self-improvement should consist of the following things:

    1. Knowledge of self-control techniques and principles.
    2. Charts and graph paper.
    3. Plastic counter.
    4. Goals and objectives.
    5. An ability to arrange the environment.

6. A desire to want to improve and change yourself.
7. The self-control to start a self-improvement program.

What do you want from yourself? Success.

Define the goal of success so that you know what it is, how to behave to reach it, and by what means it can be obtained.

The principles of behavioral control are tools that you can use to improve yourself.

The techniques of self-control make it easier to reach your behavioral goals.

The devices (electric timers, graph paper, and plastic counters) help you to count, record, and notice your behaviors. At the end of the day you can know how many times you did something if you record it with the counter.

What is a *goal*?

Goals are defined in terms of what *you want* from yourself in terms of *self-improvement*.

Decide upon your goal and then write out an exact *personal contract* with yourself to abide by, and stay with your self-improvement program. Promise yourself that you will make a *daily* effort to practice self-control.

It is your _____ with yourself that will tend to maintain your behaviors in your self-improvement program.

Answer: *contract*

You can behave in two ways to reach your goals:
1. Do less of something. Reduce smoking behaviors.
2. Do more of something. Study more hours.

Verbal mediators in the form of self-instructions can be used to regulate your behaviors.

"I will study for one hour."

Self-instructions in your personal contract with yourself will aid in the attainment of your _____.

Answer: *goals*

Restrict in *gradual* steps the *times* and *places* that you engage in unwanted behaviors.

Each day do less and less of that behavior.

Increase in _____ steps the times and places that you want to engage in behaviors.
Answer: *gradual*
Each day do more and more of that behavior.

Do not expect to alter the habits of a lifetime by a sudden change—establish a gradual pattern of change that is *reinforced* as you make progress toward the goal you have established for yourself.

Self-reinforcement can maintain and modify your behaviors.

Self-reinforcing operations are employed to provide immediate help for *self-control* of your behaviors.

Thoughts and images may act to *reinforce* your desires.

Psychologists have shown us that the learning of self-control is best whenever a complex task is divided into smaller *steps*, each of which is *reinforced* with something pleasurable.

Record your daily self-control progress and *you will become that improved person that you often dream about yourself being.*

Notes and references

CHAPTER 2

1. A. J. Bachrach, W. J. Erwin, and J. P. Mohr. "The Control of Eating Behavior in an Anorexic by Operant Conditioning Techniques." In L. Ullmann and L. P. Krasner (Eds.), *Case Studies in Behavior Modification*. New York: Holt, Rinehart, and Winston, 1965, 153–156.
2. P. R. Fuller. "Operant Conditioning of a Vegetative Human Organism." *American Journal of Psychology*, 1949, 62, 587–590.

CHAPTER 4

1. E. Coué, *Self-Mastery by Conscious Auto-Suggestion*. Cincinnati: Kantaire Publishing Company, 1923; and, E. Coué and J. L. Orton, *Conscious Autosuggestion*. New York: D. Appleton and Company, 1924.
2. W. Isaacs, J. Thomas, and I. Goldiamond, "Application of Operant Conditioning to Reinstate Verbal Behavior in Psychotics." *Journal of Speech and Hearing Disorders*, 1960, 25, 8–12.

CHAPTER 5

1. Albert Bandura and B. Perloff. "Relative Efficacy of Self-Monitored and Externally Imposed Reinforcement Systems." *Journal of Personality and Social Psychology,* 1967, *7,* 111–116.

CHAPTER 6

1. T. G. Stampfl and D. J. Lewis, "Essentials of Implosive Therapy: A Learning Theory-Based Psychodynamic Behavioral Therapy." *Journal of Abnormal Psychology.* 1967, *66,* 496–503.
2. T. Ayllon, "Intensive Treatment of Psychotic Behavior by Stimulus Satiation and Food Reinforcement." *Behavior Research and Therapy,* 1963, *1,* 53–61.
3. L. E. Homme, "Perspectives in Psychology: XXIV. Control of Coverants, the Operants of the Mind." *Psychological Record,* 1965, *15,* 501–511.
4. B. H. Barrett, "Reduction in the Rate of Multiple Tics by Free Operant Conditioning Methods." *Journal of Nervous and Mental Disease,* 1962, *135,* 187–195.

CHAPTER 7

1. A. Bandura and C. J. Kupers, "Transmission of Patterns of Self-Reinforcement through Modeling." *Journal of Abnormal and Social Psychology,* 1964, *69,* 1–9; and, A. Bandura, "Behavioral Modifications through Modeling Procedures." In L. Krasner and L. P. Ullmann (Eds.), *Research in Behavior Modification.* New York: Holt, Rinehart, and Winston, 1965, pp. 310–340.

CHAPTER 8

1. P. Lowinger and S. Dobie, "What Makes the Placebo Work?" *Archives of General Psychiatry,* 1969, *20,* 84.
2. S. B. Friedman, R. Ader, and L. A. Glasgow, "Effects of Psychological Stress in Adult Mice Inoculated with Coxsackie B Viruses." *Psychosomatic Medicine,* 1965, *27,* 361–368.
3. J. E. Brody, "When Illness Follows a 'Giving Up.'" *New York Times,* April 7, 1968, sec. E., p. 11.
4. H. Benson, D. Shapiro, B. Tursky, and G. E. Schwartz,

"Decreased Systolic Blood Pressure through Operant Conditioning Techniques in Patients with Essential Hypertension." *Science,* 1971, *173,* 740–742.

5. M. J. Rosenberg, "Some Limits of Dissonance: Toward a Differentiated View of Counter-Attitudinal Performance." In S. Feldman (Ed.), *Cognitive Consistency,* New York: Academic Press, 1966, 135–170.

6. P. E. Breer and E. A. Locke. *Task Experience as a Source of Attitudes.* Homewood, Ill.: Dorsey, 1965.

Chapter 9

1. J. V. Basmajian, "Control and Training of Individual Motor Units." *Science,* 1963, *141,* 440–441.

There is much literature in the area of biofeedback. The following are good general books that describe the area well.

Marilyn Ferguson, *The Brain Revolution: The Frontiers of Mind Research.* New York: Taplinger Publishing Company, 1973.

Gerald Jonas, *Visceral Learning: Toward a Science of Self-Control.* New York: Viking Press, 1973.

Jodi Lawrence, *Alpha Brain Waves.* New York: Avon Books, 1972.

Chapter 10

1. J. Wolpe, "The Systematic Desensitization Treatment of Neuroses." *Journal of Nervous and Mental Disease,* 1961, *132,* 189–203. J. Wolpe, *The Practice of Behavior Therapy.* New York: Pergamon, 1969.

2. J. Wolpe and A. A. Lazarus, *Behavior Therapy Techniques.* New York: Pergamon, 1966.

3. Ibid.

4. G. L. Paul, "Two-Year Follow-Up of Systematic Desensitization in Therapy Groups." *Journal of Abnormal Psychology,* 1968, *73,* 119–130.

5. G. D. MacClean and R. W. Graff, "Behavioral Bibliotherapy: A Simple Home Remedy for Fears." *Psychotherapy,* 1970, *7,* 118–119.

6. B. Migler and J. Wolpe, "Automated Self-Desensitization: A Case Report." *Behavior Research and Therapy,* 1967, *5,* 133–135.

Chapter 11

1. "Electrosleep Relaxes Patients for Therapy." *Science News Letter,* September 22, 1962, 192; C. Solomon, "The Russians' New Sleep Machine." *This Week,* January 13, 1963, 5–64.

Chapter 12

1. Both of these articles appeared in B. Ghiselin (Ed.), *The Creative Process: A Symposium.* Berkeley, Calif.: University of California Press, 1952.
2. A Bandura. *Principles of Behavior Modification.* New York: Holt, Rinehart and Winston, 1969, p. 623. This book does an excellent job of presenting the principles of modifying behavior, and it would be useful in the further development of your self-control program.
3. L. E. Homme. "Perspectives in Psychology: XXIV. Control of Coverants, the Operants of the Mind." *Psychological Record,* 1965, *15,* 501–511.
4. J. S. Livingston. "Myth of the Well-Educated Manager." *Harvard Business Review,* January-February, 1971, 79–89.
5. K. E. Schnelle, *Case Analysis and Business Problem Solving.* New York: McGraw-Hill Book Company, 1967.
6. P. Sagon, "MIT Hopes to Make Itself the Mother of Salable Inventions." *The Wall Street Journal,* January 2, 1975, 1 and 2.
7. A. F. Osborn, *Principles and Procedures of Creative Thinking.* New York: Charles Scribner's Sons, 1953.
8. R. P. Crawford, *Direct Creativity, with Attribute Listing.* Wells, Vermont: Fraser Publishing Company, 1964.
9. C. H. Clare, *Brainstorming: The Dynamic Way to Create Successful Ideas.* New York: Doubleday, 1958.
10. F. Zwicky, *Discovery, Invention, Research.* New York: Macmillan Company, 1969.

11. C. R. O'Neal, "Morphological Analysis." *Business Horizons*, December 1970, 48–58.

12. A. M. Green, E. Green, and E. D. Walters, "Voluntary Control of Internal States: Psychological and Physiological." *Journal of Transpersonal Psychology*, 1970, 2, 1–28.

CHAPTER 13

1. L. P. Ullmann and L. Krasner (Eds.), *Case Studies in Behavior Modification*. New York: Holt, Rinehart, and Winston, 1965.

2. D. Premack, "Reinforcement Theory." In D. Levine (Ed.), *Nebraska Symposium on Motivation: 1965*. Lincoln: University of Nebraska Press, 1965, 123–180.

3. A. Richardson, *Mental Imagery*. New York: Springer Publishing Company, 1969.

4. B. R. Bugelski, *The Psychology of Learning Applied to Teaching*. New York: Bobbs-Merrill Company, 1971.

5. Many of the ideas for improving one's studying can be found in Lungberg Fox's article, "Effecting the Use of Efficient Study Habits." *Journal of Mathematics*, 1962, *1*, 75–86.

Good memory books are: H. Lorayne, *How to Develop a Super-Power Memory*, New York: Frederick Fell, 1972; and T. G. Madsen, *How to Stop Forgetting and Start Remembering*. Provo, Utah: Brigham Young University Press, 1968.

CHAPTER 15

1. M. B. Harris, "A Self-Directed Program for Weight Control." *Journal of Abnormal Psychology*, 1969, *74*, 263–270.

Index

Actions, 133
Aesthetic susceptibility, 125, 126
Air pollution, 75
Alcohol, 90
Alpha
    creativity, 130
    machines, 89, 90
    rhythms, 89, 90
Alternatives, 48
Analysis paralysis, 126
Anorexia nervosa, 11
Anxiety
    fears and phobias, 91–103
    measured, 96
    and sleeping problems, 118
Asthma, 74–76
    biofeedback and, 89
Attitudes, 15, 17, 18
    toward life, 80

Attribute listing, 129
Autonomic functions, self-control of, 85
Autosuggestion, 26
Aversive stimuli, 50, 51, 70
Ayllon, T., 52

Bachrach, A. J., 11
Bandura, A., 37, 38
Barrett, B. H., 54
Base line, 27
    for reading, 139
    for weight, 156
Behavior, 24, 25–26
    controlled, 55
    environment, 60
    recognition of, 25
    restricting, 56, 160
    study of, 137

Behavior modification, 3, 4, 5, 85
  aesthetic susceptibility, 125
  calculus, 116
  personality, 17
  phobias, 93
  salesmanship, 150–51
  shaping, 37, 40
  weight control, 158
  writing, 140
Biofeedback, 86, 107
  anxiety, 96
  creativity, 130
  high blood pressure, 79
  imagery, 130
Biological control, 86–89
Biological monitoring, 85–90
Brain rhythms, 89–90
  alpha, 89, 90, 130
  beta, 89
  delta, 89
  theta, 89, 90
Brainstorming, 129
Breer, P. E., 80–81
Bugelski, B. R., 134

Caffeine, 90, 156
Calculus, 115–17
Charting, 34–35
Chevreul Pendulum method of hypnosis, 110
Classical conditioning, 3
Coffee and brain waves, 90
Cognitive, 3
Common cold, 74
Competing response, 56
  and smoking, 160
Comprehension (reading), 139–40
Concentration, 109–15, 132–33
  memory, 135
  self-hypnosis, 110–17
Confinement, 55
Consequences, 9
  aversive, 50, 51, 156–57
  shaping behavior, 59
Consistent efforts, 32–33
Contingencies, 39–41
  aversive, 47, 48, 159–60
  management, 39, 40
  memory, 135
  money, 50
  reinforcements, 40
  self-education, 138
  thinking, 128, 133
  writing, 142
Contract, 27–31, 166
  copy of, 29–30
  memory, 135
  personal, 27–31, 132
  success, 148
  writing, 143
Control, 12–14, 163
Coué, Emil, 26
Coverants, 126
Covert desensitization, 157
Covert sensitization, 53
Creativity
  biofeedback, 89
  development and control of, 122–24
  environment, 122–24, 128, 130
  problem solving, 126, 127

process, 127
techniques, 128–30
tension, 128
and thinking, 121–22, 132

Daydreaming, 52, 89
Deadlines, 128
Desensitization, 94–96
Dewey, J., *How We Think*, 133–34
Diet, 77, 154, 155
Direct action, 20
Dislikes, 48, 50
Diving reflex, 79

Eating behavior, 154–59
Education, 63, 138
Electrosone, 119
Emotional reaction, 48, 49, 51, 80
Environment, 40, 51, 59, 63
  aversive, 62–64
  contingencies, 159, 161
  creativity, 122–24, 128, 130
  criminal, 64
  gambling, 65
  habits, 153–54
  intellect, 132, 133
  memory, 135
  Skinner Box, 64–66
  sleep, 119
  social, 63–64
  stress, 76
  studying, 136
  thinking, 133
  vocational, 63
Excessive controls, 12–14

Extinction, 51

Fears, 91–103
Feedback, 35
Flying, fear of, 99–103
Food, 154
Free association, 92
Friedman, S. B., 74
Fuller, P. R., 12

Goals, 28, 29, 36, 132, 133, 142, 143, 166
Gradual changes, 33–34, 166, 167
Guidelines for self-control, 26

Habits, 11, 153–61
  covert sensitization, 53
  daydreaming, 52
  eating, 154–59
  and environment, 153–54
  nail-biting, 126
  smoking, 159
  unhappiness, 18
Harris, Mary, 157–59
Headaches, 88–89
Health, 71, 72
Heart disease, 77
High blood pressure, 77–79, 87–88
Hypnogogic imagery, 89, 130
Hypnosis, 95
Hypochondria, 71

Ideas, 126
Imagination and self-reinforcement, 51

Imitation, 68–69
Implosive therapy, 51
Incompatible responses, 56
Insomnia, 119
Intellect
  creative use of, 131–36
  and environment, 133
  and memory, 135
  modifying, 132

Learning, 3, 33, 133, 134, 135
  sleep, 117–19

MacClean, G. D., 97
Memory, 10, 135–36
Migraines, 78
Models, 69
Motivation, 16–18, 109, 135

Nail-biting, 1, 26
Negative cognitions, 125
Negative reinforcements, 27, 47, 48
Nervous twitch, 54
Neuroses, 92
Noise, 62
North Dakota, University of, 101

Obstacles, 55, 160
Operant conditioning, 4, 9
  learning, 134, 138–39
  levels, 27
  phobias, 94
  writing, 142
Osborn, A. F., *Principles and Procedures of Creative Thinking*, 128

Painting, 26–27
Patient, as therapist, 96–98
Pavlov, Ivan, 3, 51
Penfield, W., 10
Peptic ulcer, 72
Permanent effects, 10–11
Personality, 17, 18
Phobias, 91–103
Physiology, 76, 106
Placebos, 73–74
Pleasure, 38–39
Poincaré, H., 124
Positive consequences, 57
Positive reinforcer, 39
Power, 11–12
Practice, 27
Principles of self-control, 23–36, 47, 158–59, 164–65
Problem solving, 20, 90, 132
Procrastination, 18–21
  and salesmanship, 150
  and success, 148–49
  and writing, 141, 144
Programmed learning, 138–39
Psychosomatic illness, 71
Psychotherapy, 92
Punishment, 49–50, 156, 160
Purpose, 148

Reading, 139–40
Reinforcement, 35, 38–39, 167
  environment, 159
  intellect, 133
  learning, 134, 135

negative, 27, 47, 48, 50
positive, 39
procrastination, 19
salesmanship, 151
schedules of, 41, 42, 43, 44, 52
shaping, 31
smoking, 159
tools for, 69–70
Relaxation, 105–7
blood pressure, 78
phobias, 93, 95
self-hypnosis, 108–17
therapy, 78
Repetition
autosuggestion, 26
memory, 135
Response, 3
Restricting behaviors, 56, 160
Rewards, 37–40, 48, 51, 143

Salesmanship, 149–51
Satiation, 52–54
Schedules of reinforcement, 38, 41–45
intermittent, 42
interval, 42
variable, 43, 44
Schizophrenia, 31
Self-contract, 19
Self-control, 1, 20, 37
behaviors, 24
environment, 59
habits, 153
program for, 165–67
salesmanship, 150–51
sleeping, 118
smoking, 159–61
weight control, 157–59
writing, 140–44
Self-education, 138
Self-generated motivation, 16
Self-hypnosis, 108–17
method for inducing, 110–15·
Self-instructions, 166
Self-reinforcements, 38, 45, 125, 134, 167
imagination and, 51
Shaping, 31–32, 40
Skinner, B. F., 60
Skinner Box, 64–66
Sleep
environment for, 119
learning, 117–19
Smoking, 5, 26, 52, 159–61
Social environment, 63–64
Speed reading, 139–40
Spender, S., 124
Stimulus, 154
Stimulus control, 67, 72
Stress, 74, 75, 76–77
biofeedback, 87
Studying, 27, 136–38
Subconscious mind, 26, 35, 108
Success, 166
Symbolic operants, 126
Symbolically produced consequences, 51
Symptom substitution, 93
Systematic desensitization, 94–96, 157

Talking, 98

Tension, 106–7
  creativity, 128
  headaches, 78
Thoughts and thinking, 24, 118, 132, 133, 167
  controlling, 53
  environment, 133
  skills and drills, 133

Ulcers, 76–77

Variable schedules of reinforcement, 43
Verbal mediators, 166
Vocational environment, 63

Watson, John, 4, 92
Weight, 26, 157–59
White noise, 62, 109
Withdrawal of reinforcement, 54–55
Wolpe, J., 94, 96
Work environment, 81
Writing, 140–44
  goals, 143
  operant conditioning of, 142

Yoga, 107
You, 7, 14, 165

Zen, 87